East Anglian Disasters

East Anglian Disasters

GLENDA GOULDEN

First published in Great Britain in 2011 by
Wharncliffe Local History
an imprint of
Pen & Sword Books Ltd
47 Church Street
Barnsley
South Yorkshire
S70 2AS

Copyright © Glenda Goulden, 2011

ISBN 978 1 84563 120 8

The right of Glenda Goulden to be identified as author of this work has been
asserted by her in accordance with the Copyright, Designs and Patents Act 1988.

A CIP catalogue record for this book is available from the British Library.

Printed and bound in England by
CPI UK

Pen & Sword Books Ltd incorporates the Imprints of
Pen & Sword Aviation, Pen & Sword Maritime, Pen & Sword Military,
Wharncliffe Local History, Pen and Sword Select, Pen and Sword Military Classics,
Leo Cooper, Remember When, Seaforth Publishing and Frontline Publishing.

For a complete list of Pen & Sword titles please contact
PEN & SWORD BOOKS LIMITED
47 Church Street, Barnsley, South Yorkshire, S70 2AS, England
E-mail: enquiries@pen-and-sword.co.uk
Website: www.pen-and-sword.co.uk

Contents

Acknowledgements

The counties of Suffolk, Norfolk, Cambridgeshire, Huntingdonshire and Essex have excellent libraries, record offices and museums. I used the archive material held by many of them and found their staffs knowledgeable and helpful, and always interested in East Anglia, its present and its past.

Of special value were those in Newmarket, Norwich, Great Yarmouth, King's Lynn, Cambridge, Saffron Walden, Huntingdon, Ipswich and the University Library, University of Cambridge.

I received particular information from the National Railway Museum (York), the National Maritime Museum (Greenwich), the Time and Tide Museum (Great Yarmouth), the Imperial War Museum (Duxford and London), the RNLI (Harwich), the RAF Air Historical Branch, University of Cambridge Department of Architecture and the Cambridgeshire Collection of Cambridge Central Library.

I am grateful to Rupert Harding of Pen and Sword Books Ltd for his interest and advice.

List of Illustrations

Introduction

Robinson Crusoe, the castaway hero of Daniel Defoe's famous 1719 novel, sailed from Yarmouth Roads to begin his adventure, but he had gone only a few miles along the Norfolk coast to Winterton when his ship was wrecked in a North Sea storm typical of that stretch of sea.

In 1692, in what became known as the Great Gale, 200 vessels were lost in one night at Winterton. In a severe north-easterly gale 140 were driven ashore and wrecked with the loss of over 1,000 crewmen. The masses of floating wreckage and bodies became hazards in themselves. A disaster of its day, widely reported, that incident may have given Defoe the idea that was to lead to the start of *Robinson Crusoe*.

The treacherous nature of that part of the coast was made obvious to him when he toured parts of East Anglia in 1722. Despite rights of wreck belonging, in most places, either to the Crown or to the Lord of the Manor, he found that the local people were skilled salvagers, filling storehouses with whatever came their way, and making use of every bit of the wrecks themselves. He wrote that there was not 'scarce a barn or a shed, or a stable, nay, not the pales of their yards and gardens, not a hogstye, not a necessary house, but what was built of old planks, beams, wales and timbers etc, the wrecks of ships and the ruins of mariners' and merchants' fortunes'.

Charles Dickens discovered a less stormy Great Yarmouth when he spent some time at the Royal Hotel in Marine Parade in the 1840s and his hero, David Copperfield, found the bustling resort 'upon the whole, the finest place in the universe'. Dickens had first visited East Anglia in 1836 as a young reporter for the *Morning Chronicle*. For over two decades after that he regularly visited the area. Mr Pickwick, in *Pickwick Papers*, stayed at the *Great White Horse*, Ipswich, and *The Angel*, Bury St Edmunds, both hotels that Dickens himself stayed at in 1859 and 1861.

A century later, more than two centuries after Defoe's visit to East

Anglia, Arthur Ransome was writing his series of children's adventure stories. Ransome, of an East Anglian family of Quakers, had two geographical loves – the Lake District and the watery parts of East Anglia. At one time he lived at Leverington, on the river Orwell, and between 1932 and 1940 five of his stories – *Peter Duck, Coot Club, We Didn't Mean to Go to Sea, Secret Water* and *The Big Six* – had settings in Norfolk, Suffolk and Essex.

Eric Blair, who lived at Southwold in the 1930s, took his pen name, George Orwell, from that of the river when he wrote his political satires, *Animal Farm* and *Nineteen Eighty Four*, and he set *The Clergyman's Daughter* partly in Southwold.

They, and many other authors, who have lived in or visited East Anglia have been drawn by its uniqueness and often have been inspired to make it an important part of their writing. They have looked over its far horizons, wet and dry, known its life, its heritage and its people, and have been inspired to create exciting fantasy. But East Anglia's reality has been as colourful.

Hereward the Wake and his band of dispossessed Anglo–Saxons defied the conquering Normans at the island abbey of Ely in the eleventh century, while in the seventeenth Oliver Cromwell of Huntingdon, always an East Anglian, fought a Civil War to take the throne from Charles I and become the Lord Protector of England. Even in death not all of him left his home region. His head remains in Sidney Sussex, his old college in Cambridge.

There had been no need to create fictional heroes when the great eighteenth century navigator explorer, George Vancouver, was a King's Lynn man, and in Burnham Thorpe was born 'the greatest sailor since the world began', Admiral Horatio Nelson, one of East Anglia's most celebrated sons by the time of his death in the Battle of Trafalgar of 1805.

In the early years of the nineteenth century, Madame Marie Tussaud brought her travelling waxworks exhibition to East Anglia with, alongside effigies of notorious criminals, casts of the heads of aristocrats guillotined in that most continental of disasters the French Revolution. Unable to return to France because of the England-France War, she toured fairs in Suffolk and Cambridgeshire until she found a permanent location in Baker Street, London.

But East Anglia, over the centuries, had had disasters of its own. Its history could tell of that as plainly as imported replicas of severed heads, popular though they were with the penny-paying crowds.

The earliest of those disasters, other than ravaging incursions by the sea, were invasions by foreign forces. The penalty for being close to mainland Europe and Scandinavia was that successively, from the Celts to the Romans in the first century AD, the Vikings of the ninth century to the Normans of the Conquest in the eleventh, the region was obliged to play host. It was 1667 before the last enemy force landed in Suffolk, when the Dutch attacked Landguard Fort. A feared Napoleonic invasion at the start of the nineteenth century never came, but east coast armed defences against the threat were built in 1809. The seventeen Martello towers can still be seen along the coast, between Shotley and Aldeburgh, at points where an invading army could most easily have been landed ashore. Some are now used by coastguard services.

Christian from the seventh century, a religion propagated by St Felix of Burgundy, the 'Apostle of the East Angles', many monastic houses became established in the region, at Bury St Edmunds, Ely, Peterborough and other places in the fenland. Most were sacked by the Danes in the ninth century and the smaller ones went out of existence. Others recovered to accumulate great wealth and estates until, after the arrival of the Normans, there were at least eighty thriving in East Anglia.

The Normans rebuilt churches plundered by the Danes and, as something of a public relations exercise, they enhanced them with massive towers. Sadly, catastrophe was built into them. Many of the region's churches and cathedrals suffered disasters, retold here, but none can have been as spectacular as those of the towers. They dropped like Fred Dibnah's chimneys. There were structural failures at Bury and Peterborough, but the collapse of the central tower at Ely in 1322 led to triumph over calamity as an Octagon was erected in its place to become the glory of the cathedral.

The Romans had fed their army throughout Britain on the corn grown in East Anglia on what was appreciated, even then, as prime agricultural land. They made the first attempts at fen drainage and created the first artificial waterway to carry the region's produce to their legions in other areas and, in doing so, tried, to make farmers of some of the native Iceni. They made only an enemy of their queen, Bouddica, who told her men, 'You have learned the difference between foreign tyranny and the free life of your ancestors', as she led them in revolt against Roman rule. She lost, and took her own life. Tyranny, as she had seen it, won.

But for tyranny in the sixteenth century the monasteries needed to look no further than the king – Henry VIII. In amassing their vast estates the region's religious foundations had become rich and acquired far more power than Henry liked. They would have to go. In 1553 came the first Act for the dissolution of the monasteries in England and their estates fell into the hands of self-enriching 'new men'. In many instances, while sheep and wool increasingly ruled the nation's economy and created wealth for the few, they enclosed common land and made agricultural labourers subservient and poor.

In a rising against their plight, led by Robert Kett of Wymondham, 20,000 men marched on Norwich. Kett is considered one of Norfolk's heroes for inspiring the labourers to lay siege to the great city and to make their demands known but, as was usual in a popular rising, with never a real hope of success. Some 3,000 died, most of them the men who put food on the family table, however meagre. A disaster for many an innocent Norfolk family, and for the desolated city of Norwich.

The Great Fire of London of 1666, following the Great Plague, is a well-known historical event. But catastrophic town fires were commonplace at that time. Almost every town and large village burned in an age of open hearths and lighted candles when most buildings were of inflammable timber and thatch and fire precautions and the means of fighting fires were basic.

In Suffolk there were devastating fires at Beccles, Bungay, Bury St Edmunds, Debenham and Brandon. Most were rebuilt, but at Southwold, a prosperous fishing port badly damaged in a fire of 1659, there was no rebuilding. Seven greens were created instead of housing in the burned-out areas. Half of the racing town of Newmarket was destroyed in a fire of 1683 but, a good thing or a bad depending on allegiance, it saved the life of the king, Charles II. Resident in his palace across the High Street from the blaze, he was in little danger. But the smoke was more than he could bear. He left for London several days earlier than expected and so thwarted a planned ambush and assassination attempt at Rye House.

There was a fire of a different kind in the Cam-side village of Burwell in 1727 when a puppeteer bound for Cambridge's Stourbridge Fair, the greatest annual fair in Europe, stopped to put on a show in a barn. An unexpected penny treat for the villagers. Stacked with straw trusses and roofed with tons of dry reed thatch it took only one lighted candle to turn the makeshift theatre into a box of flame. Eighty-one people, many of them children, died.

Even today, in an age of advanced navigational aids and weather forecasting, disasters still occur off the East Anglian coast in the notoriously stormy waters of the North Sea. Today the loss of one vessel is a disaster, but in the past numbers beyond count were lost, caught up in the violence of storm, running aground on shifting sandbanks or driven ashore by wind and tide. At the end of the nineteenth century there were so many wrecks on the beach at Happisburgh that Trinity House, with the power to remove or destroy non-Royal Navy shipwrecks, cleared them with explosives.

Traffic of merchant ships and colliers in the sea lanes was as heavy as that on a Bank Holiday motorway and fishing boats added to the congestion with, in the early years of the twentieth century, as many as 1,000 putting out from Yarmouth alone in the herring season in search of the 'silver darlings'.

All who worked aboard vessels knew of the dangers and were the first, before the first official lifeboats, to risk their lives to save others, often coming by valuable salvage as they did so. And sometimes, perhaps in answer to prayer, they did not even need to put to sea to find it. There was the bonanza, on their doorstep, and it was an ill wind indeed that blew nobody a bit of good. A prayer of a vicar of St Mary's in the Scilly Isles, asking the Lord to bless all sailors, would end, 'But if it is Thy divine will that their ship shall be lost, then, we pray Thee, let it happen on our coast.' It was a sentiment to which many an East Anglian would say 'Amen'.

And their prayers were more than answered when, in a snow-driven gale on 24 February 1837, the steamer *Raby Castle* was wrecked on the shore close to Cley-next-the-Sea. Despite high seas, her seven crew and two passengers reached safety in the longboat. It was when the ship began to break up and shed her cargo of oranges, nuts, tea and spirits, then worth £5,000, that the fun began.

According to the *Norfolk Chronicle*, by seven o'clock in the morning there were 300 people on the beach. By eight o'clock there were 600, and then 'the most outrageous and beastly conduct was exhibited'.

Some barrels of spirits were buried in the sand for later recovery while others were broached and people collected the spirits in whatever container they had to hand – in most cases their oilskin hats or their shoes. The outcome was inevitable. 'Many men were conveyed from off the beach dead drunk and it is with disgust we add many women were in the same state.'

Some vicars of coastal churches, besides offering up prayers, may not question the occasional drop of something from a wreck coming their way. Others would try to prevent the wreck. Storms may have been acts of God, but they would avert the consequences if they could, placing a guiding light in their towers, visible for up to twenty miles out at sea along a flat, featureless coast, and, when that failed, burying the drowned seafarers in their churchyards. They served their communities well until the coming of the lights of Trinity House.

A lighthouse was erected at Happisburgh in 1791. Much needed but perhaps overdue. Trinity House was granted a charter by Henry VIII in 1514 to regulate pilotage on the Thames, its powers extended by Elizabeth I in 1566 to include the placing of sea-marks. They took a long time to reach all parts of one of the most dangerous coasts in Britain.

An historic wreck off Happisburgh in 1801 was that of HMS *Invincible*, sailing to join Nelson's fleet for the Battle of Copenhagen. Aground on a sandbank, battered by gale and waves, she broke up, drowning 400 men, 119 of them later buried in Happisburgh churchyard, the resting place of others, before and after them, who fought the North Sea and lost.

In 1845 death by water struck seventy-nine of the inhabitants of Great Yarmouth as, like those in Burwell, they had been eagerly anticipating entertainment. A circus was in town and to advertise it a clown was to sail along the Bure in a washtub pulled by four harnessed geese.

People, many of them children, crowded onto a suspension bridge. They pressed to one side for a better view of the spectacle as it approached and the bridge collapsed, throwing them into the river to their deaths. The bridge had been about to be replaced by a more substantial structure able to carry the increased traffic which had come with the recently opened railway station at Vauxhall.

Railways changed life in East Anglia, as they did everywhere, helping to establish the region's seaside resorts while carrying passengers, goods and mail quickly, cheaply and safely.

Safely until, on single-track lines, at Thorpe in September 1874 and Barnby at Christmas 1892 there were head-on collisions caused by fog and human error. Snow and ice caused the crash of the famous *Flying Scotsman* at Abbots Ripton in January 1876, but its derailment at Conington in March 1967 was not caused by the weather. It took a court case to decide if there had been error, human or inhuman. It was

believed that a young signalman, deliberately or by accident, had opened
a set of points as the express was speeding over them. Had he?

With nowhere in East Anglia more than fifty miles from the coast and
its counties crossed by rivers and waterways, water, salt or fresh, is a
feature of many people's lives, today as in the past. There is a constant
danger, given certain weather conditions, that parts of the region could
suffer serious flooding.

The stories of three quite different twentieth century floods are told
here, beginning with 1912 when excessive rain deluged the region and
caused the Wensum to burst its banks to flood Norwich. In 1947, after a
hard winter of snow and ice followed by a thaw and rain, the Fens were
inundated by a sudden inrush of water from beyond the region, and in
1953 there came the worst peacetime disaster in British history. During
the night of 31 January, in hurricane conditions, a tidal surge hit the
entire length of the east coast. It resulted in the deaths of 307 people,
most of them in Essex and Norfolk. Over 40,000 were evacuated and
150,000 acres of agricultural land were flooded – and the same, or worse,
could happen again at any time despite heightened defences.

Almost everywhere in Britain suffered some level of disaster in the
two World Wars. East Anglia, with the proximity to continental Europe
which had brought past invaders, was again a target for bomb-carrying
German airships in the First World War, the first time that civilians
anywhere had had to experience airborne warfare. The first ever
fatalities caused by attack from the air were in Great Yarmouth early in
1915, while a Zeppelin shot down at Theberton in June 1917 was the last
to be destroyed over Britain.

Harwich harbour and approaches, from before the seventeenth
century, was often the arena for East Anglia's war at sea. In the Second
World War German mines became a particular threat and in just four
days in November 1939, in the earliest weeks of the war, three ships
were mined and sunk with high loss of life – a Japanese and a Dutch
passenger vessel and a Royal Navy destroyer,

In the air, the Zeppelin had been surpassed by the long-range bomber.
Many East Anglian towns were bombed in the Second World War, some
repeatedly, and often more than once on the same day. On 21 February
1941, Great Yarmouth had been raided four times by just after
lunchtime and on 11 May 1953 eighteen German planes made a low-
level attack just as breakfast was on the table, 'indiscriminately bombing
residential areas at the north end of the town'. One bomb destroyed

most of the town's Seymour Avenue.

Only three days later it was the turn of Newmarket. In what was a one-off, afternoon attack on the Suffolk racing town, a single Dornier dropped ten bombs and some incendiaries along a High Street crowded with market day shoppers, machine gunning as it went. Twenty-seven were killed and many were injured in one of the worst incidents in East Anglia.

As the war progressed, many civilians died but the first anywhere in mainland Britain had been Mr and Mrs Frederick Gill when a mine-laying Heinkel crashed onto their home in Victoria Road, Clacton, on 30 April 1940.

Along with other cities listed as 'of significant historical interest' in the German *Baedeker* guide book for tourists to Britain, Norwich was bombed in what became known as the Baedeker Blitz. On two nights at the end of April 1942, 297 high explosive bombs and thousands of incendiaries were dropped, killing 231 people, and more raids were to follow. Thousands of people began to 'trekk', leaving their homes in the city each night to sleep in the surrounding countryside, perhaps showing East Anglian caution rather than cowardice. Morale was not broken, boosted by a visit from King George VI from nearby Sandringham, even if the city was.

Broken but, by the gallantry of four men escaping total destruction, was the small Cambridgeshire town of Soham. On 2 June 1944, just four days before D-Day, the first wagon on a long train of bombs was found to be on fire. The engine's fireman uncoupled the burning wagon and, with assistance from guard and signalman, it was driven away from the rest of the train before it exploded. Both the engine driver and fireman received the George Medal, the only time that two railwaymen have received it for the same incident.

Many of the airfields which had been set up throughout East Anglia during the war remained after its end, developed for USAF and RAF use, their location most vital while the Cold War threat lasted.

One such airfield was RAF Wyton, near Huntingdon, which became a base for photo-reconnaissance Canberras. Disaster was unavoidable when, on 3 May 1977, a returning Canberra, on its flight path over the Oxmoor housing estate, went out of control. It crashed, spreading burning fuel over a terrace of houses, killing three children and the plane's crew of two. By not ejecting the crew gave their lives to save an adjacent school. The accident, bad as it was, had narrowly missed being much worse and led to questions of why there were flights over a housing estate and whether housing should have been built beneath an already existing flight path.

Where there are stretches of water people need to cross them. Ferries for centuries crossed East Anglia's rivers, sometimes failing to reach the other side. There was a tragic river ferry disaster on the Cam in Cambridge in 1905, over two centuries after lives were lost on an Ouse ferry in King's Lynn. Ferries also crossed the sea, to and from the continent, facing war and waves, and there were accidents, but it was with ROROs that a new kind of disaster came.

The development of roll-on roll-off vessels was originally for military use but, in 1953, they were introduced as passenger and vehicle ferries. In the build-up to the tidal surge which was to devastate East Anglia at the end of January 1953, the rail ferry *Princess Victoria* became the first civilian RORO to be lost, sunk in the Irish Sea when her stern doors failed. Other accidents followed, sometimes due to design shortcomings of that type of vessel, one being the likelihood of her being swamped by water breaking through a bow or stern door. But in December 1982 a serious RORO accident was due to the collision of two ferries in a safe, wide channel between sandbanks off Felixstowe. In a cold midnight gale the European Gateway capsized in ten minutes, bringing death in peacetime to six men in waters which had for centuries held the dead of war.

Here, then, are the fascinating accounts of very different disasters which have coloured the history of East Anglia. They tell of life in the region, as it was and as it is, and most of them could have happened nowhere else.

Chapter 1

In the Name of the Lord

During a visit to Poppyland, the area between Sheringham and Sidestrom popularized as Victoria's reign came to an end as a genteel holiday destination for the artistic, the theatrical and the literary, Sir Arthur Conan Doyle was told the legend of Black Shuck. One of East Anglia's oldest and most horrifying myths is that of a large black devil dog the size of a calf or a donkey, ranging and raging through lonely places, from marsh to fen to restless shore, to claim the souls of the unaware. He was so fascinated by the legend that he was inspired to write *The Hound of the Baskervilles*, published in 1902.

But it was no legend to the people of Blythburgh as they attended service at Holy Trinity church on the morning of Sunday, 4 August 1577.

For a village, Holy Trinity was an immense church. It had been built over eighty years in the fifteenth century when Blythburgh had been a flourishing town, trading in wool and fish, where the river Blyth was tidal. But the river had silted, the trade had gone elsewhere, and the town had declined to become a village. Only Holy Trinity, the Cathedral of the Marshes, dominating the tranquillity of the once-lively estuary, was a reminder of lost grandeur.

There was a violent storm over Suffolk that morning. And rain such as no one had seen before. Still there was the usual full congregation, listening to the reading of the Second Lesson, when lightning struck the steeple sending it crashing through the roof and into the nave. It shattered the font, killing two worshippers, but an early account tells of something rather different.

Whatever had happened had 'cleft the door and, returning to the steeple, rent the timber, brake the chimes and fled towards Bongay six miles off.'

It cleft the door? It returned to the steeple? And it fled? Did lightning do that? Not in Blythburgh. Everyone there knew at once that the Devil had been at work in Holy Trinity. The Devil in the guise of Black Shuck, with slavering jaws, saucer-sized eyes of fire and the smell, not of old dog, but of brimstone.

And he had been seen. One man wrote that after returning to the steeple Black Shuck had stood on a beam over the rood screen and then 'sodainly he gave a swinge down through ye churche, and there also, as before, slew two men and a lad, and burned the hand of another that was there among the rest of the company, of whom divers were blasted. This mischief thus wrought, he flew with wonderful force to no little fear of the assembly, and out of the church in a hideous and hellish likeness.'

He left marks on the north door as he left. They may have seemed like scorch marks made by lightning, but the people of Blythburgh knew better. They were scratches made by Black Shuck's fearsome claws as he stormed out, on his way to petrify another congregation in St Mary's, Bungay.

As the storm rocked and rolled over Bungay the congregation in St Mary's suddenly saw Black Shuck racing down the nave. Forcing his way between two people as they prayed he 'wrung the necks of the bothe at one instant clene backward, in so much that even at a moment where they kneeled they strangely dyed'.

Another man managed to escape death even though Black Shuck 'gave him such a gripe on the back that there withall he was presently drawen together and shrunk up, as it were a peece of lether scorched in a hot fire, or as the mouth of a purse or bag drawen together with a string'. Even as the lightning flashed the Devil was there, in canine form, in St Mary's.

The Devil was as real as God in sixteenth-century East Anglian lives, and stayed so real that eighteenth and nineteenth century smugglers, especially around Cley, used the legend of Black Shuck to keep villagers away from their haunts. Even today there are some believers in the satanic dog and sightings are reported.

East Anglian churches, their towers and steeples often the highest point in the flatness of the surrounding landscape, were struck by lightning on numerous occasions. Even the finest church in Suffolk, Holy Trinity at Long Melford, built in the late fifteenth century as an expression of the wealth of local clothiers, including John Clopton of Kentwell Hall, felt the power of the heavens. Its tower was struck by lightning in 1709, but there was no mention of the Devil there. Clothiers, men of enterprise and substance, were too practical for that. They just got on with the business of rebuilding.

Neither was there talk of the Devil in one Norfolk church. Oh no. Its congregation was far less gullible than its Suffolk counterparts. Worshippers knew exactly what had happened when lightning struck the tower of Morston village church, thirteen miles west of Cromer, in 1743. It was a sign that the Second Coming of Christ was about to take place. They were so sure of it that they did not repair the damage caused to the church and tower. There was no need. Christ was coming again and they would be with Him in glory – and a brand new church. It was many disappointed years later before the tower was patched up. Which was more than happened where Black Shuck had carried out that demonic act of his in Blythburgh.

Holy Trinity was left to crumble aided in 1644, during the Civil War, by a visit from the Puritan zealot, William Dowsing. Dowsing, a Suffolk man, born in Laxfield, took it upon himself to clear 150 Suffolk churches of their stained glass, brasses, statues and other relics of popery – and he did the same in Cambridgeshire. At Blythburgh, he and his men used Holy Trinity as stabling for their horses, smashed its windows and church ornaments, and used the wooden angels in its roof for target practice.

What was left of Holy Trinity after Dowsing's efforts remained unrepaired until, in 1880, the windows bricked up and the whole building on its way to total ruin, the congregation – yes, its worshippers were staunch, they were still there – had to shelter under umbrellas as rain poured through holes in the roof. And that became a turning point. It was decided, with Victorian resolve, that something must be done and restoration began the next year.

It was still going on during the Second World War when, on Saturday, 12 August 1944, there was an almighty bang. Not the return of Black shuck but the explosion of United States bomber overhead loosening the windows and shaking Holy Trinity to its ancient foundations. The modified B-24 Liberator, codenamed Anvil, was carrying out the first mission in Operation Aphrodite, for which the plane had been made, in effect, a guided missile, a robot, packed with 21,000lb of Topex explosives. The two-man crew was to parachute, leaving it to fly on to its target, on that occasion the V-3 cannon site at Mimoyecques in France. But, due to an undetermined electrical malfunction, detonation took place ten minutes early with the crew still on board. Its pilot, a volunteer for what his citation for posthumous award of the Navy Cross, the Distinguished Flying Cross and the Air Medal called 'an exceptionally hazardous and special operational mission', had been Lieutenant Joseph Patrick Kennedy of the United States Naval Air Service, elder brother of future United States president Jack, who became the inheritor of the political destiny which had been expected to be his. Lieutenant Kennedy was vaporised in the blast. By a seemingly fateful chance, in a de Havilland Mosquito just 100 yards behind the Liberator, filming the mission, had been Colonel Elliott Roosevelt, son of the then United States president, Franklin D Roosevelt. His Mosquito, although damaged, made it back to RAF Fersfield.

It was another United States statesman, Benjamin Franklin, who saved at least one East Anglian church from disaster. Franklin, a keen inventor, began researching electricity in 1746. He proved that lightning and electricity were identical and devised the lightning conductor for the protection of buildings.

On 9 November 1927, the parish church of Cromer, St Peter and St Paul's, was struck by lightning during a severe storm. At about ten-thirty that night a terrific explosion sent people rushing out into the dark, cold streets despite the teeming rain.

Flames were seen coming from the ground in front of a side porch of the church and the fire brigade was called. Once the fire was put out it was found that the lightning conductor on the church tower had done its job, directing the electricity into the ground and saving the building.

The bang had been so loud that it had alarmed the whole town, and crew members had taken it as the signal to launch the lifeboat. But it was the church that had been saved.

Not so fortunate was St Mary's in Happisburgh. On a hazardous coast, with the dangerous Haisboro Sands just a few miles offshore, the 110ft tower of the church, visible from far out at sea, served as a landmark. To make it even more visible, of even greater value to seafarers, a large wooden cross was put on the top of it. When that was blown down in a gale in 1818 its even larger replacement had Ben Franklin's invention attached, which 'served as a conductor for the electric fluid'.

And lightning did strike it in 1822. The result, however, would have appalled Mr Franklin, as it did the people of Happisburgh. The cross became a cross of fire. It collapsed, taking part of the tower with it to crash through the roof of the aisle. The church caught fire but, by good fortune, it was not completely destroyed.

The cross, perhaps with the safety of the church in mind, was not replaced. But it was no longer needed. By then the seamen of Happisburgh, thanks to the work of Trinity House, had a light.

It was possibly due to its lightning conductor that Norwich cathedral was not damaged when it was struck by lightning early in the morning of 18 September 1992, but that had not always been the case. Lightning first hit the cathedral on 29 June 1271, St Peter and St Paul's Day, as the abbey's monks were at prayer. They were unhurt, but 'two pillars were struck down'.

The cathedral's original wooden spire was destroyed in a hurricane in 1362. It was replaced by a 315ft spire, completed in 1480. All was well until 29 April 1601 when a storm 'caused a great darkness' followed by hail, thunder, lightning and 'a noisome stink of brimstone' as the spire was struck, knocking off its top.

In 1643 the timber spire on a central tower was struck by lightning and the roof of the nave, not for the first time, went up in flames. Around 1170 the nave's wooden roof had been destroyed by fire. And it burned again in 1272, an outcome of a bitter quarrel between the prior and monks and the men of Norwich over the prior's right to impose tolls on a local fair. The prior armed his monks and engaged mercenary soldiers to lead a pillaging attack on the city. The men of the city responded by throwing burning missiles into the monastery and onto the cathedral roof. A lovely blaze and, again, no roof.

It was a tribute to the builders of Norwich cathedral, other than Durham, the most completely Norman structure in the country and evidence that Norman masons could build to last, that it survived so many potential disasters without any major damage and continued to do so through the repeated German raids of both the First and the Second World War.

Not all East Anglia's cathedrals, or abbey churches as some of them were before elevation, escaped catastrophe, and some of them were fated to suffer on more than one occasion.

From the arrival in the kingdom of the East Angles of a Burgundian missionary monk, Felix, brought to Dunwich by the Christian King Sigbert in AD 672-673, the region became rich in religious establishments. Sigbert himself founded a monastery at what was to become Bury St Edmunds. Others were founded at Norwich, Ely and Peterborough. A first cathedral of the See of East Anglia was built at Dunwich, with Felix serving as its bishop.

The many abbeys and monasteries became powerhouses of their local economies and important centres of learning, skilled crafts, culture and accumulated wealth. When a great force of Scandinavian fighting men landed in East Anglia in 865, bent on robbery, pillage and destruction, it was on the monasteries and churches that they directed their savagery. In 870 they struck, not at their spirituality, but their prosperity.

Using a waterway as access, a monastery founded by St Felix at Soham was sacked. Ely, in the fastness of the fens, was plundered, as was Bury St Edmunds. Peterborough was demolished and its abbot and monks killed, the first in a succession of calamities to befall it. Peterborough would be sacked again by Hereward the Wake in 1070 and burned in 1116, said on that occasion to have been by a servant who had called on the Devil to kindle some firewood.

The ravages of the Danes were so great that it seemed certain that the region's monastic life would not survive, and for more than a century it barely did so, but then along came King Edgar. In 954 he founded a new abbey at Ramsey and restored the two great fenland minsters, at Ely in 966 and Peterborough in 970.

The monasteries next test of faith came in the years after the Norman Conquest of 1066 arising not out of destruction by the new invaders but from their urge to build. William the Conqueror saw the erection and extension of religious buildings throughout the land as proof of his good kingship. From the great abbeys of Normandy he brought his own abbots to run existing monasteries, mostly Benedictine, and soon established new orders, such as Cluniac, Cistercian and Augustinian.

From Normandy, too, came the church builders, masons skilled in stonework, and from Caen came the stone they were to shape into Romanesque splendour. They did it on a large scale. Their towers alone were of massive proportions, giving the appearance of solidity and durability, as they rose to eminence. The century after the Norman Conquest was one of headlong church construction and extension and, during that period, most of the monastery at Ely was built. In 1109 it was made a bishopric and the abbey church became a cathedral. Peterborough became one of the grandest of all Norman abbey churches as through the twelfth century, from 1118, much of the present cathedral was built. Norwich cathedral became the first and largest Norman building in Norfolk.

For some time, into the thirteenth century, it seemed that East Anglia's religious establishments had much to be thankful to William for. The monasteries had Norman abbots foisted upon them, some good and some bad, but their buildings were sound and their churches, some raised to cathedral status, were a celebration of the Conqueror's largesse.

And then it all began to fall apart. Literally. It began in Bury St Edmunds in 1210 where the original timber church had been demolished and a great stone abbey church built over twenty-nine years. When completed, with its vast central tower and two smaller octagonal towers with spires, it was larger than most cathedrals, including Norwich, and could accommodate an extra sixty monks.

On 23 September 1210, either a calm day or a windy day, depending on the chronicler, the central tower fell. An omen of worse to come.

In 1322 it was the turn of Ely. On the night of 12–13 February the cathedral's central Norman tower fell with a crash so resounding as to 'make the whole city to tremble and to cause men to think that an earthquake had taken place'. There had been concerns for some time about the stability of the tower. The choir beneath it was not being used and the monks were using St Catherine's Chapel, at the end of the south transept, for prayers. But still, bravely, they would go to and from beneath the tower. On the fateful day, they had processed from the chapel to the shrine of St Erminilda and back again and had just retired, when down it came.

Alan of Walsingham, sacrist at the time and responsible for the fabric of the building, was distraught, not knowing what to do at first. And then he got going. He had the stones and rubbish cleared away and foundations for a replacement dug. His vision had become clear and he knew exactly what he wanted for his cathedral. Eight columns began to rise and building began on the Octagon and Lantern, today the glory of Ely and 'one of the surviving miracles of the Middle Ages'.

The collapse of the tower at Ely had the monks of Peterborough saying extra prayers for the stability of their own Norman tower. They were convinced that it was insecure. They became so worried about it that, in the 1330s, they pulled it down.

The turn of Bury St Edmunds again. Now the western tower fell, but not all at once. It performed an architectural striptease. The south side came down on 18 December 1430 and the east side on 30 December

1431. The remaining north and west sides were gingerly taken down in 1432 before they could fall. The reason for the collapse, it was decided, was 'excessive ringing of the bells'.

Towers had become popular because of the need to house bells and bell ringers but, as today, the clamour of the bells was not appreciated by everyone. At Bury the bell ringers were blamed. Too much clamour of those blessed bells and see what had happened! But were the bells to blame? The crash of the tower at Ely might almost have been heard in Bury. And there had been other disasters of a similar nature where no bell had been rung.

In church after abbey after cathedral, in East Anglia and beyond, Norman towers, and especially those built over crossings, were dropping. In the words of one historian, 'they dropped like ninepins'. William had had pride in his masons. They had built magnificence in Normandy. He had brought them to England to build the same. What had gone wrong?

How about pressure? They had been given a great amount of building to do in the shortest time possible. So many builders had been needed that semi-skilled and unskilled labour had been pressed into service. The builders, building in haste, paid too little attention to the stress being exerted on piers, pillars and arches beneath the towers. And those massive piers were not as solid as they seemed. Cutting corners, making up for the scarcity of stone and avoiding the arduous task of dressing the stone that they had, they packed the piers with rubble, carelessly filled in and grouted.

And all of that was on top of dodgy foundations. In that respect, the jerry builder's gold medal must go to whoever was responsible for the tower at Peterborough. There, after it had so wisely been dismantled, it was found that the piers, the entire tower, stood on loose rubbish. There had been no foundations when, just three feet down, there had been solid rock.

Norwich escaped disaster, perhaps because it had been a completely new build, overseen by the master masons William thought so highly of and employing the most skilled men. Norwich lost only a wooden spire – and it took a hurricane to shift that!

No builder was responsible for what happened at Dunwich, where St Felix had become the first bishop of East Anglia and established a centre of learning and Christianity. He believed that God had sent him from Burgundy to 'preach the word of life to the nation of the Angles' – and that he was to do it from Dunwich.

It was not the best location that either God or Felix could have chosen. Dunwich became a focal point for East Anglian religion. Abbeys, monasteries, hospitals, churches, chapels and a cathedral were founded there, and none of their many founders, it seems, read the signs that Dunwich was the worst place to build so much as a sandcastle.

One of the earliest churches to be built, perhaps the first in what had become a sizeable town in which master mariners, burgesses and merchants jostled with the more spiritually minded, was that of St Felix. It was the first to fall into the sea, at the end of the twelfth century.

It can hardly have been a surprise. The cliffs of Dunwich were sandy. The sea, funnelling down the North Sea to meet the upward thrust from the English Channel, scoured constantly, wearing away the base of the cliffs to create an overhang which could only lead to collapse. The process, hastened by fierce storms and tidal surges, was relentless. And it always had been. The Roman settlement of Dunwich had crashed onto the seabed, and the same fate had awaited the Saxon city, the medieval port and the Dunwich that became the capital of East Anglia.

An entry in the Domesday Book of 1086 tells the tale of the manor of Dunwich, held by Robert Malet, It had been reduced from two carucates of land to one. 'The sea carried away the other.'

Already the sea had taken its toll. William, apparently, knew of that, because, building everywhere else, he made no attempt to build so much as a privy at Dunwich. Others, less aware, did and had to deal with the consequences. Here are just some in a catalogue of Dunwich disasters.

St Anthony's chapel, built close to the sea and the church of St Felix in the twelfth century, ceased to exist. In a severe storm in 1286 'the sea overtook a third of Dunwich', blocking the harbour and sweeping away three parishes and three churches, but it was one night of storm in January 1326, when one million tons of shingle and sand were deposited in the harbour mouth, diverting the river Blyth, that ended the town's trade and began the exodus of merchants and residents. Meanwhile, its religious buildings were fighting and losing battles of their own.

In 1300 St Bartholemew's, a 'grand building', stood near the sea. Sadly, it was too near. It was lost in 1332, just three years before the tall-spired St Martin's was abandoned and lost. The church of St Nicholas was abandoned in 1352. It fell piecemeal and it was 1740 before the last remains of its cemetery were washed away. St Leonard's, built in the twelfth century, did not linger. When it was its turn to go, it went, lost to the sea about 1385, the same year in which Blackfriars monastery, judiciously built well away from the sea, found that the waves were lapping at its door.

In the sixteenth century St Francis' chapel went into the sea, as did St Katharine's, followed by the most important and largest church in Dunwich, St John's. Ominously, that church was near to the market place in the centre of town. Not a good sign for the town and its future. As soon as St John's became threatened and, with it, Dunwich itself, parishioners tried to protect it, to delay its destruction, by building a wall. But in 1540 it became obvious that no wall would be enough to hold back the sea and St John's was dismantled before it could fall. St Peter's in north Dunwich was a fine church famous for its stained glass and memorial brasses. The chancel went first, in 1688. Half of the steeple followed it over the cliffs in 1697. There was time for the bells and anything else of value to be removed before the other half went over in 1702.

The round church of the Knights Templar, dedicated to the Virgin Mary and St John the Baptist, stood on high ground to the south of All Saints' church in the twelfth century. It was a church of great wealth, property and privilege, but that did not prevent it dropping onto the beach in the mid-seventeenth century – of course after the astute knights had removed what valuables it had held.

Its neighbour, All Saints, was the last church of any significance to be lost in Dunwich, the last in the town's sad rosary of disasters. It was in normal use until 1754, and then continued to be used for baptisms, marriages and funerals despite the creeping ever closer of the cliff edge. Gradually, it became a ruin, a skeletal structure on the top of the cliffs, and it was as late as 1923 before, to save a remnant of it, the last corner of its tower was moved to the churchyard of the still surviving St James. A solitary gravestone at the cliff edge was all that remained.

The small village that Dunwich became, perched tenaciously above the crumbling cliffs, continued to be threatened by the sea - and no one blamed Black Shuck. The cliffs continued to crumble and, as they took church after church, they also took their graveyards. Bones stuck out of the cliff face. Each time another slice crashed down skeletons lay on the beach.

On 8 April 1904, a *Daily Chronicle* reporter wrote of Dunwich: 'Dismembered fragments of the bodies of those who were once its proud citizens now cumber the beach and make playthings for the waves of the North Sea.' A landslip occurred while he was there and dozens of gaunt bones protruded from the earth and sand. He wrote then: 'I counted a score of fragments of human limbs, there a thigh bone, there a part of a pelvis, and there, perched on a mound of earth and masonry, a broken toothless skull, the sockets where the eyes had been staring out on the restless waters.'

Over a hundred years later, some bones may still be there, a poignant present-day reminder of the long and glorious, yet at times tormented, history of Christianity in East Anglia.

Chapter 2

A Popular Rising

Edward VI, when he became king in 1547 at the age of nine after the death of his father, Henry VIII, inherited a changing and turbulent kingdom. Because of his age, the Duke of Somerset, the brother of Jane Seymour and the young king's uncle, was appointed Protector to rule the country with a King's Council until Edward was old enough to rule alone.

By 1549 England had undergone the Reformation and the Book of Common Prayer of the Church of England, written in English by Thomas Cranmer, the Archbishop of Canterbury, was about to be published for the first time.

The years leading up to it had been coloured by Henry VIII repeatedly marrying, the dissolution of the monasteries, war with France and Scotland, and union with Wales. But the lives of rural labourers, as the feudal Middle Ages neared their end, were more affected by what was taking place in their own back yard – or common field.

Since the end of the fifteenth century, many landowners, as the price of wool rose, had been changing from growing crops to raising sheep, requiring less labour at less cost. That was especially so in East Anglia. While the meat was readily sold it was the wool that brought in the real profit at home and abroad, either as the raw product or woven into cloth.

The pursuit of gain took over and, despite various Tudor governments trying to stop them, sheep farmers began to take over and amalgamate the land of several small farms into one, taking out fences and hedges to form pasture. They also took the common land which traditionally had been at the disposal of the labourers, allowing them to farm and to keep a cow, pig or a few sheep to bolster their already borderline existence. As it was taken and enclosed many lost their jobs, their subsistence and often their homes.

On 1 June 1548 Protector Somerset issued a Proclamation on behalf of Edward VI and his Council condemning enclosures because 'of late by the enclosing of lands and arable grounds, in divers and sundry places of the Realm, many have been driven to extreme poverty, and compelled to leave the places where they were born, and to seek them living in other countries, with great misery and poverty insomuch that whereas in time past in some places a hundred or two hundred Christian people hath been inhabiting and kept household now there is nothing but sheep or bullocks.' Instead of many families at work on the land there may be 'one poor shepherd', with everyone else 'driven from their houses by sheep'.

He made it clear that the ten-year-old king 'by advice of his most entirely beloved uncle, the Duke of Somerset' felt that it was time for an inquiry to be made into all enclosures and the practices which had arisen from them through the 'greedy covetousness of some men' leaving everyone else 'eaten up and devoured by brute beasts'. Commissioners were to be appointed to receive information of offences so that 'a convenient and speedy reformation might be made herein to the honour of God and the King's Majesty and the wealth and benefit of the whole Realm'.

So – enclosures were denounced by Royal Proclamation and it seemed to the suffering peasantry of England that Protector Somerset had their well-being at heart. He offered them hope against the landowners. Within a few weeks commissioners were sent to several counties, with Bedfordshire and Northamptonshire the nearest they got to East Anglia, to inquire about the number of acres enclosed or converted to pasture since 1485 and to find out who kept more than 2,000 sheep. They presented their findings in a Petition to Parliament against the landowners and enclosures and for the labourers who had been impoverished.

Good old Somerset. It was all going to change. The labourers were to come into their own, as was their right. But – Parliament took no action. It ignored the whole thing, as did the landlords, who carried on as before, incensed by Somerset's interference, while the thoughts of the labourers turned from restless disquiet to riot.

Somerset was alarmed. He realised that he had made a serious mistake. He had made personal enemies among the gentry and landowners, and they were the people whose support he relied on to maintain his position and status. That wouldn't do. So he ordered another Commission in the spring of 1549, and that one, in an about face, was to enforce enclosures.

Labourers throughout England were, by then, 'plucking down poles, hedges and ditches at their pleasure' and Somerset, keen to appease the offended landlords, could not condone it. But, not quite forsaking his former backing of the lower orders, he declared that he would pardon 'the great number of rude and ignorant people who had done great and most perilous and heinous disorder, and had riotously assembled themselves, who repented of their evil doings'.

An advisor, Sir William Paget, warned him in a letter that such lenience was misguided. 'Your pardons have given evil men a boldness to enterprise and cause them to think you dare not meddle with them, but are glad to please them and to suffer whatsoever they list, and what pleaseth them, be it right or wrong, they must have it.' Of 'these matters of tumult' he advised that twenty or thirty of the 'rankest knaves' should be taken and 'let six be hanged, the ripest of them, the rest remain in prison'.

Whether Somerset would have taken that advise or not was never determined because by the time that he was in receipt of that letter the great Norfolk rising, the tumult above all other tumults that he would have to contend with, had begun, encouraged by mention of pardon and a mistaken belief that the Protector, who spoke on behalf of the King, was at heart with the labourers and against the landowners. It was too late for a re-think.

The rising began at Attleborough on 20 June 1549 where John Green, lord of the manor of Wilby, had erected fences and hedges around common lands in Harpham and Attleborough. They were pulled down by local labourers.

But what next? The men were ready, eager, to be an effective rising, but they had no leader and lacked organisation. What should they do? 'At first, therefore, were secret meetings of men running hither and thither, and then withdrawing themselves for secret conferences, but at length they all began to deal tumultuously and to rage openly.' Still they lacked direction.

Two weeks later, on Sunday, 7 July, the annual feast in honour of the Festival of St Thomas of Canterbury was held in Wymondham, six miles from Attleborough. A chapel in the town was dedicated to him. Crowds from a wide area around congregated in the town on the Saturday. There was to be a church play and a fair, an occasion which would entail a coming-together of many people suffering the effects of the enclosures going on around them. The opportunity was there for arousal, and aroused they were.

Were they just to put up with it? People in Attleborough had torn down Squire Green's fences - and why not? They had just cause, and Protector Somerset would forgive them. Gaining courage and purpose from each other at the feast, a band of Wymondham men marched three miles to the village of Morley where they demolished some fences, and then they marched six miles in the opposite direction to pull down fences belonging to Sergeant Flowerdew, a Hetherset lawyer, who had enclosed common lands.

Flowerdew, even before his enclosures, had been unpopular with the people of Wymondham. In the late 1530s, when Henry VIII had ordered the destruction of Wymondham Abbey, the people had petitioned the King to save the abbey church, which served as the parish church. He had agreed. At a price. They must pay for anything of value, such as bells and lead. They had found the money and had paid, but along had come Flowerdew and taken the things that they had paid for.

Principal amongst those hoping to save the church had been the members of a prosperous, landowning family – the Ketts. Despite some relationship through marriage between them, resentment had flared and had continued. Flowerdew would harm the Ketts when he could. The Wymondham mob had pulled down his fences. So, he thought, the Ketts should suffer the same. They had enclosed land as he had. He bribed the mob, said to have been with forty pence, to go back to Wymondham and destroy the fences of Robert Kett. Had he not done so the disturbance may have fizzled out, ended when the feast did. But they took his pence and they did as he asked.

The Ketts were a long-established lower gentry Norfolk family dating back to the time of King John. Robert Kett, in 1549, was a fifty-seven-year-old tanner and landowner, a wealthy family man living a comfortable life. He had not suffered the privations of the times and had no reason to feel ill done by. It is hard to understand why, therefore, when the mob began to take down his fences, he helped them. He joined in the uprising.

When the rioters, along with some of their wives, reassembled the next morning to march the nine miles to Norwich to demonstrate their grievances it was with a direction and purpose that they had lacked before. Through Flowerdew they had found what they had lacked. A leader. When the march began it was led by Robert Kett. Without him there would have been no march on Norwich. What was to come was because of Kett.

Norfolk authorities were at once alarmed. They sent an appeal for help to members of the local gentry, Sir Roger Townshend and Sir William Paston, and to the King at Windsor. What had begun as a small local disturbance had become, as the number of marchers quickly grew, a regional and national anxiety. Paston sent two cannon to Norwich from his home at Caister.

As Kett skirted the city he gathered more followers, many of them Norwich's poorest citizens, as hard-pressed as the rural labourers. They made camp at Bowthorpe, two miles from the city, where some fences were pulled down to keep their hand in. Sir Edmund Wyndham of Felbrigg, the High Sheriff of Norfolk and Suffolk, arrived to proclaim them rebels and to order them, in the King's name, to disperse. The answer was 'no.' Other local somebodies called at the camp, including the Mayor of Norwich, Thomas Codd. They all made the same pleas, and got the same reply. But the city's disaffected, turning up in increasing numbers, were welcome, as were the weapons they brought with them. All believed that their demands for their old, lost rights were just and that, in Somerset's name if not the King's, they should and would be exonerated.

They continued, crossing the Wensum. At Hellesdon, there was Sir Roger Wodehouse of Kimberley to meet them. His was a fresh approach. He had with him two cartloads of beer and provisions. They could take them – if they would disperse. They did not disperse, but they took them anyway, and took Sir Roger prisoner.

Still they went on, reaching Sprowston on the fourth day. There they destroyed the dovecote of John Corbet, a Norfolk lawyer. The rebels did not like pigeons kept by the gentry. It was an upper-class pastime. But Kett was set on more than the destruction of a few doves.

From there he and his rag-tag army, his 'parcel of vagabonds', reached what was to be their base for as long as the rebellion lasted – the high and wooded Mousehold Heath. He set up his headquarters in a mansion, Surrey House, and a hastily concocted mish-mash of Twenty-nine Demands was put together and sent to the King. The issues of enclosures, prices and rents were prominent, but a surprising number of demands, perhaps in the aftermath of the Reformation, were about offences committed by 'parsons and vicars'. And, of course, the keeping of doves was opposed. And the keeping of rabbits. But fishing was good. There was to be river fishing for all and, perhaps to widen their appeal to coastal Norfolk, they asked the King that 'poor mariners and fishermen may have the whole profits of their fishings as porpoises, grampuses, whales or any great fish so it be not prejudicial to Your Grace'. Today's fishermen would appreciate such champions!

Side issues apart, it was proven in those demands that the rebellion was about the classes as they then were, high and low, far apart from each other in the realities of their lives. The force of town and country labourers was opposing the county's landowners, and any who may hold sway over them, and Kett was about to show whether he possessed the qualities needed to lead such a band of men to the achievement of their aims. But, as they entrenched themselves on Mousehold Heath, it may be considered if it would have been better if he had not. Historically, no matter how just the cause, the small man did not win against the big man. Was Kett, marching at the head of an ever-increasing mass of followers, an East Anglian Pied Piper, only leading them to disaster and death? He had begun with about 2,600 in his band. In a matter of three or four days that had risen to 20,000. And all were malcontents, itching for action. They would not wait long.

The increasing numbers alarmed the Corporation of Norwich. An appeal for military help was made to the King's Council while Kett set about organising his vast camp, finding food, money and arms. From beneath a tree, the Oak of Reformation, he held court and issued orders. He was joined by Mayor Codd and three or four other city dignitaries, 'not because they favoured his plans or approved the revolt, but because they hoped to keep the rebels from excesses, and by their influence prevent an attack on the city'. Kett also chose two men from every Hundred in the county to add their names in support of his Demands.

The King's response to Kett's list of demands was delivered by a herald who pointed out that a proclamation had already been issued against high food prices and that commissioners were carrying out a 'reformation of enclosures and of divers other things'. They would arrange the reduction of rents and the price of wool. Rebellion would do nothing to help matters. The King's advice was that they should 'apply themselves to their harvest and other peaceable business at home, and not to drive him to necessity (whereof he would be sorry), by sharper means, to maintain both his own dignity and the common quiet'. And, true to Somerset's word, he also brought a general pardon, 'in case they would quietly desist and disperse'. They did not do so. By then they believed that their actions were legitimate and therefore they did not need pardon.

Codd stayed with Kett for nine days, each day hoping for an answer to the message he had sent to London asking for help to prevent a disaster, the destruction of Norwich. If he had hoped for troops to end the rising he was disappointed. What turned up was another herald bringing another pardon which he read to a turbulent crowd at the Oak of Reformation. He ordered 'that they forsake the camp and this den of thieves, and everyone to depart to his own house'. A few did. But Kett answered for the mass of his followers when he told the herald, 'Kings and princes are wont to pardon wicked persons, not innocent and just men. We, for our part, have deserved nothing and are guilty to ourselves of no crime, and therefore we despise such speeches as idle and unprofitable to our business. I trust I have done nothing but what belongs to the duty of a true subject.' The cheers of the crowd told the herald that he had failed.

When he left, Codd went with him. The city was locked and Codd 'caused good watch and ward to be kept in especial at the dangerous places'. An attack by Kett was expected at any moment. Both sides armed, the city with at least ten cannon. That evening, 21 July, the first shots were fired.

The next day the rebels tried to storm several of the city gates. 'With loud cries they rushed down the hill upon the city, but were withstood every way and especially by bowmen.' There was a windstorm of arrows, but all was not lost if some lives were. 'At Bishopsgate the river was swum and entry forced into the city. The gunner placed there fled. Others, seeing that, did the same. The rest that watched, seeing themselves nothing to resist, also hastily departed.' Kett had the city.

The herald – the fellow had guts – went to the market place and made a further appeal to the rebels to 'lay down their arms, leave the camp, depart severally to their own homes, and rely on the mercy and pity which the King was so ready to show them'. If they refused they could expect only 'grievous torments, bitter death and all extremity'.

'Depart with a plague on thee!' was the excited mob's response. They had just won a city. The Corporation paid the herald £4 in gold, escorted him to St Stephen's Gate and saw him on his way back to London. When Codd and several aldermen were taken back to Mousehold Heath that evening it was as the rebels' prisoners, 'where they remained in chains, and some died'.

On 29 July Kett heard that Lord Northampton was on his way from London with an army to put down the rising. He reached Norwich on 31

July. No herald that time. If their answer was to be 'no' yet again they must fight for it.

With Northampton were Lords Sheffield and Wentworth. Amongst the accompanying knights was Sir Thomas Paston. They led about 1,500 troops, including Italian mercenaries, and the message sent to Kett was that he must yield or be at war. Northampton was confident that he would put down the rising quickly. Kett's army, so called, was no more than 'a bunch of vagabonds' and would be overcome without trouble. The vagabonds, however, had other ideas.

Fighting began that evening, a skirmish between some mercenaries and rebels on Magdalen Hill. Several of Northampton's men were taken prisoner and one Italian nobleman, in Kett's absence, was hanged by 'a wretched rebel, one Cayme of Bungay'. Kett would not have allowed it. He had stressed that there were to be no hangings or executions, but he shared the indignation of his men that foreign mercenaries had been brought in to prevent Englishmen seeking freedom.

That night, to ward off the darkness, Northampton's men made a huge bonfire in the market place. But no fire could have prevented their overwhelming by Kett's much larger force. The rebels stormed down from Mousehold Heath 'as a running stream' and surged into the city. Desperate, bloody fighting lasted for three hours. At its end 300 rebels lay dead, the price of riot, but they had fought well, leaving Northampton with his confidence shaken, knowing that his troops were too few. But what could he do? He soon thought of an answer. Send a herald with a pardon.

A herald was sent to the Rockthorpe Gate on the morning of 1 August. No one was there. Hard to proclaim to nobody. A trumpet was blown. A few rebels came down from the hill. With them was John Flatman of Beccles who told the herald - and Northampton - what he could do with his pardon:

> I care not a pin's point for my lord Marquis of Northampton, who is a man neither of courage, counsel, nor good fortune. I despise him and hate him as an infamous and worthless man.

That told him. And, as it did, a cry went up and the herald realised why so few rebels had come to hear him. The rest were attacking the city again. Fighting was fierce in Tombland and around Bishopsgate and the cathedral. Lord Sheffield was unhorsed, fell into a ditch, and was butchered, an easy task for Fulke, a butcher by trade. The rebels charged on all sides and Northampton's army fled. It fled the city, fled back to London and, it must be presumed, to Italy. The battle was over in time for lunch and Northampton was gone.

Kett was in control of Norwich for three weeks. He was fair and firm, no lives were threatened and women were respected, but the city's situation was bad. There was a lot of praying going on.

He had sent word of the success of his rising far and wide, hoping to lead a rising of all the suffering people in England, but, disappointingly, there was little response, even in Norfolk. As a last desperate attempt he sent 100 men to Yarmouth – he had thought of its fishermen in his Twenty-Nine Demands - but Yarmouth did not want to know. It sent three burgesses to London to tell the King. Somerset, in a reply of 6 August, said that he would 'very shortly and by main force weed and try out our good subjects from the evil'. Another army was to be sent against Kett, and he would lead it. Until it arrived they were to keep Yarmouth out of his hands.

They did. If Kett wanted Yarmouth it would have to be taken by force. His men stormed the walls of Yarmouth on 17 August but were beaten back. Their next attack was from Gorleston, 'intending to bother the town from thence'. It was a mistake. Townsmen set fire to a large stack of hay and the smoke engulfed the rebels. Thirty were taken prisoner and many were killed as they came under attack. That ended Kett's seaside excursion and his hopes of a Norfolk-wide rebellion. All he was to have was Mousehold Heath.

Somerset began mustering his army on 10 August but, always careful to look out for himself, decided that he could not lead it 'without alienating the popular support which his domestic policy had brought him.'. His army of 12,000 men with, that time, mercenaries from Germany, was to be led by the Earl of Warwick.

By 20 August it was at Cambridge. Northampton was not a soldier. Warwick believed that he was. He was tough. There would be no leniency from him, no offer of pardon. The rising of a bunch of Norfolk nobodies had been allowed to go on too long. He would destroy Kett. Warwick's army was at Wymondham on 22 August and, a day later, on the outskirts of Norwich.

On 24 August Warwick sent a herald ahead of him with a demand that the city gates should be opened to him or there would be war. Kett sent two of his prisoners, city aldermen, Augustine Steward and Robert

Rugg, to meet the herald at St Stephen's Gate and ask him his business. If Kett was not afraid of Warwick's army, ten times the size of Northampton's, they were. And they grovelled. Declaring that 'they counted themselves the miserablest men alive', they regretted that circumstances prevented them being loyal to the King, as they wished, and begged Warwick to again offer pardons to all rebels who would disperse. They wanted peace without slaughter and bloodshed.

That was Warwick's idea too. The less bloodshed the better. He decided, after all, to offer pardon. St Stephen's Gate was opened and the herald, a trumpeter, the two aldermen and thirty-five mounted rebels went to Bishop's Gate Bridge, near Kett's camp. The trumpet sounded and 'great routs of rebels came flocking by heaps unto them from the hill'. The crowd was so large that it spread over quarter of a mile.

The herald delivered his speech. A long one. Mercy and pardon did come into it, but there was much more about riotous lusts, horrible pollutions of wickedness, destruction and slaughter. And the King wanted an end to it. He had told Warwick not to leave off until he had 'utterly rooted out that vile and horrible company'.

The crowd was more roused than cowed. It was hostile. A boy made a rude gesture, as boys so often do. He showed his bare bottom to the herald, and that was the catalyst to all out war. A soldier fired an arrow at the boy and shot him dead. The crowd became a mob, threatening the herald, but peace, he managed to say, could still be negotiated if Kett and Warwick were to meet, man to man. Kett considered it. Already many of his men had been injured or killed. The rebellion had not spread. Was it time to end it? His men, however, begged him not to yield and became such a riotous horde that even the herald, afraid for his life, begged him 'to go back again and stay this concourse and tumult' rather than see Warwick. He did.

There had almost been a truce, an end. Kett had been willing. The rebels, whose fate he had at heart, had not. The herald went back to tell Warwick. Kett and his men got ready for the fight of their lives.

The killing of some of the rebels already in the city began while Warwick's main army made its way to the market place. There Warwick hanged sixty rebels. On the afternoon of Saturday, 24 August, while the hangings went on, Warwick's guns, arms, cannons and ammunition entered Norwich by Saint Benet's Gate. But, in the unfamiliar narrow streets, the train of gun carriages got lost. Instead of turning right to reach the market place they went straight on. They went straight across the city and out again at Bishop's Gate where Kett was waiting. He took the lot.

With such an unexpected artillery bonanza the rebels were brimming with a belief in their own invincibility. They had beaten Northampton and they were well on their way to doing the same to Warwick. They began an offensive, fighting in the streets and killing Warwick's troops. When Warwick mounted a concerted attack in response, he was met, at St Andrew's, by 'a mighty force of arrows as flakes of snow in a tempest'. At least 300 on both sides were killed. And, still a prey to the rebels' guerrilla tactics, while that was taking place, the small amount of ordnance not already captured by Kett was taken from the Welsh troops left to guard it. They ran, terrified by the mass of men raining down the hill towards them armed with pitchforks, bill hooks and scythes.

Fighting resumed the next day with Warwick, despite his claims to be a warrior, comfortably billeted in Alderman Steward's house. He was taking his ease when, in mid-morning, he was told that the rebels had forced a way into the city and were setting fire to houses in Conisford Street and premises at the Common Staith, and the fire was spreading, 'for they meant to burn the whole city'. More rebels were attacking the city from the north and Warwick ordered the destruction of all bridges that would give them access.

With war in their streets the blameless citizens of Norwich wisely cowered in hiding. Even those sympathetic to Kett's cause must have despaired at the disaster being worked about them as their city was ravaged and burned. Kett had defeated Northampton and was going to defeat Warwick, but what would be left of their great city by the time that he did? Some citizens went to Warwick and 'besought him humbly, seeing that the number of his men was but few and the power of the enemy great and not to be resisted, to consult his own safety, to leave the city, and not suffer the matter to be brought to utter extremity'.

Warwick refused to leave Norwich, swearing that he 'would deliver it or leave his life', adding, 'I will first suffer fire, sword, finally all extremity, before I will bring such a stain of infamy and shame either upon myself or you'. Not what the citizens had hoped to hear, and not such brave words as they seemed. He knew that reinforcements were on the way.

They arrived the next day, Monday, 26 August – 1,400 mercenary German lanznechts, complete with lances, and their wives. They came while he was in his billet eating a good Norfolk dinner, and more than

Warwick was relieved. The city was. Warwick had refused to leave but now there was no need. There would soon be an end to Kett and to the destruction of Norwich.

Kett knew of the arrival of the lance knights. He needed to consider the new situation, to think, to make careful plans before his next move. Sadly, he did not do that. He decided quickly. And in that one moment of decision the die was cast. It was decided on that Monday morning that the entire rebel force would leave Mousehold Heath, the high wooded ground which had given them refuge and could still have been used to their advantage. They came down to a valley, Dussindale, to the north of Norwich, where the ground was level and their advantage was lost. Instead, at Dussindale, Warwick and his professional soldiers and mercenaries had the edge, and it was a sharp one. Kett's men, good country men of Norfolk, were slaughtered.

Perhaps, if Kett had taken more serious note of an omen before their departure from Mousehold Heath it would not have happened. As they prepared to leave on their fateful descent a snake 'leaping out of a rotten tree did spring directly into the bosom of Kett's wife, which thing struck not so much the hearts of many with a horrible fear as it filled Kett himself with doubtful cares'. But, apparently, not enough doubtful cares. His men were confident of victory and no plans were changed.

By Tuesday morning Kett's army was in place and Warwick and his army went to face it. At that late stage he made a last attempt to prevent battle. He appealed to the rebels to surrender. There was a pardon for all but the ringleaders. They could leave the field, there and then. Not one man did so. Warwick ordered extermination.

His cavalry at once broke through Kett's lines. His gunners 'fired their pieces with such a terrible volley of shots' that Kett's front lines bolted. The rest knew from that moment that they had no chance. They were village hicks facing trained troops. So they ran too. But they could not run from massacre.

After six weeks of triumph under inspiring leadership all was lost in six hours and Kett escaped the field through the shredded remains of those who had followed his inspiration. All was lost. The bodies of at least 3,000 were heaped high, the rising was at a bloody conclusion, but a small band of survivors made a makeshift barricade and swore to die together, fighting to the last. Warwick heard of it and for a last time a herald was sent to promise pardon if they surrendered. But rebels had already been hung in the market place and they had no belief that pardon would save them. Well, said Warwick, he would come to them and give them pardon himself. Would that do? Warwick went to the barricade. The herald read the king's pardon and they surrendered with shouts of 'God save King Edward!'

The rising was over. Hope was dead for the reform of rural injustice but Norwich could live again, could begin to recover from its wrecking. There was celebration, not war, in its streets, celebration that Robert Kett was captured eight miles away, but the killing of rebels still went on. Variously they were disembowelled alive, beheaded and quartered. Heads were 'fixed on the tops of the towers of the city, the rest of the body bestowed upon several places and set up to the terror of others'. At least 300 were hung outside Norwich and forty-nine in the market place.

The burgesses of Norwich wanted every man of the 20,000 or more who had taken part in the rising put to death, but Warwick balked at that. Rebellious as they had been, they were the men who worked the land and some, at least, must go back to it. They were needed. As Warwick pointed out to the 'rich and soft of hand' gentlemen, 'Shall we hold the plough ourselves, and harrow over our own lands?' He made his point and the executions ended.

When Warwick left for London on 7 September he took Robert and William Kett with him. Imprisoned in the Tower of London, both men pleaded guilty to the charge that they had 'made an insurrection and levied war against Our Lord the King', and were found so.

No death at Tyburn. They were returned to Norfolk to be hanged. In the cold bleakness of December Robert Kett was taken to Norwich Castle 'and then and there over the walls of the same castle, in obedience to the King's command, was hanged in chains'. At the same time, at Wymondham, William Kett was hanged in chains from the church tower. Their bodies were left until they were rotten, examples to all of the cost of agrarian revolt.

There were some men left to plough and harrow, to tend their lord's sheep, but too many good Norfolk men who kept, fed and clothed their families did not return from Norwich, from their six weeks in Kett's pitchfork army. Families were ruined and homes were lost, and the disaster of Dussindale reached to cross thousands of poor thresholds. The last great rural rising of the common people in England had ended in disastrous failure, but the question asked was had the real disaster been that it had happened at all. Should Kett have let them remain, grumbling but alive, in their own villages instead of leading them in an ill-fated attempt to escape from a servile life?

Today, many hundreds of years later, those questions answered, Robert Kett is considered one of Norfolk's heroes - even in Norwich.

Chapter 3

Fire on the Wind

When the Lord Mayor of London, Sir Thomas Bludworth, was called to see a fire soon after it had begun on Sunday, 2 September 1666, he was dismissive of it, saying, 'a woman might piss it out'. He could hardly have been more wrong. It grew to destroy 13,000 houses, many other properties and churches, and Saint Paul's Cathedral.

Worthy of the title of the Great Fire of London, it was the worst of several fires to strike the capital. But most of the towns and cities, and some of the larger villages, in England had major fires at that time. They often had more than one and when one fire was more extensive and destructive than the others it was called the Great Fire.

In Norfolk and Suffolk there were at least forty considerable town and village fires from the sixteenth century to the eighteenth and countless lesser ones. In Suffolk, between 1586 and 1789, there were Great Fires in Beccles, Bury St Edmunds, Southwold, Bungay, Debenham and Brandon. One at Newmarket threatened the life of King Charles II but, 'by God's mercy', saved it.

Let's begin with Beccles. It should be first because, amazingly disaster-prone, Beccles suffered three major fires in the sixteenth century – 1539, 1568 and, most disastrously, on 29 November 1586 – and five more in the seventeenth.

It was a windy day in November 1586, with a hard frost gripping. Just the day to stay indoors before a glowing fire. In one hearth the fire was allowed to grow too fierce. About nine o'clock in the morning it set the chimney alight and then the dwelling's thatched roof. It spread quickly through closely adjoining thatch and timber properties to destroy eighty houses, the market place and parts of the parish church of St Michael's.

The river was frozen and there was not enough water elsewhere in the town to douse the flames. With the fire running unchecked, householders saved what they could of their possessions, moving them to surrounding fields, safe from the flames. But, unfortunately, they were not safe from thieves who compounded the tragedy by stealing what had been saved.

By the time that the fire exhausted itself, at about four o'clock in the afternoon, more than £20,000 damage had been done, equivalent to £2.6 million today. Beccles needed help and Norwich was one place to respond to an appeal for financial aid in rebuilding the town, specifying that one contribution of £30-10s-8d was to go 'toward the rectifying of Beccles church which was lately burned'.

Beccles was, perhaps, a little slow in learning what precautions should be taken against fire. It was accepted that fire was the greatest menace to man's existence and its prevention was the responsibility of everyone, with arson punishable by death. There was advice for the avoidance of accidental fires despite the belief that they were acts of a vengeful God. Churches resounded with admonitions on the sinfulness of man. No wonder he was a fire-raiser! But to avert that holy retribution, people were advised on the risks to be minimised. Every home and every workplace used flame for heating, cooking, lighting or in craftsmanship at a time when most properties were made of easily combustible materials. Attention, everyone was told, must be paid to hearths, chimneys, candles, ovens, furnaces, hay, straw, corn and tobacco. The night watchman's call, 'Take care of your fire and candle!', would be heard through the dark, sleeping streets, warning that hearth fires should be damped before retiring and candles properly extinguished.

When fire did break out it often spread quickly, from thatch to thatch, along streets of closely-packed houses, too quickly to control even if a supply of water was nearby, too violently for a few buckets to be of any help at all.

It was 1656 before Beccles bought fourteen leather fire buckets, kept in the church, 'to be used when any danger of fire in the town'. And they were certainly needed. But despite the fourteen buckets further fires devastated the town in 1662, 1667, 1669, 1678 and 1689.

Thankfully, in 1711, a manual fire engine was bought and, primitive as it was, it served the town well until an improved model was acquired in 1802.

In the sixteenth century hand-held water squirts had been introduced, but they were of little more use than a bucket and had to be used dangerously close to a fire. The first fire engines, from about the 1640s, with water hand-pumped from a tank and directed onto the fire through a nozzle, were not much better. Before the introduction of hoses, the tanks had to be constantly topped-up by a chain of buckets and needed to be so near to the blaze that the engine was often set on fire and lost.

In 1608 the townspeople of Bury St Edmunds were as prepared to fight fire as they could be. Fires were too frequent in the town for them not to be. As soon as fire broke out an alarm bell was rung. That was the signal for every available cart and conveyance to be brought into use to carry barrels of water from the river Lark to the scene of the fire while men pulled down blazing thatch with long fire hooks, a common practice which could do more harm than good, sending sparks into other thatches. They did all of that on 10 April, but their all was too little.

At about half past eight o'clock in the morning fire started in Randall's malt house in Eastgate Street. Because of their furnace and kiln malt houses were always prone to fire. A careful and constant watch must be kept. There was a strong wind blowing. A wind was a contributory factor in many a major town fire from the sixteenth to the eighteenth century, speeding sparks and giving wing to flames. It did so in Bury. The flames began to consume the town. In no time at all fire reached the Market Place, half a mile from the malt house. It was fought, but nothing could prevent the whole centre of the town being burned. The lead roof of the Market Cross melted, stocks and stores of food for humans and animals were lost, and 200 houses were destroyed, making many more hundreds of the townspeople homeless and destitute.

It would take £60,000 (c.£5.9 million today) to rebuild what had gone up in smoke. To help with the rebuilding King James I, 'the wisest fool in Christendom', who had been wise enough to escape the Gunpowder Plot three years before, gave a supply of timber. But there was to be no more thatch. The town made a commendably early decision, after the fire, that only tile and slate roofing would be used in the town in future.

It was a windy, salt-in-the-air day at seaside Southwold when a blaze started over a malting on 25 April 1659. In less than four hours, three-quarters of the town was destroyed. Gone were the town hall and market house, shops, granaries, warehouses, the prison and 238 houses, 300 families were made homeless and many livelihoods were lost.

Fishing was a principal occupation in the town and Southwold's fishermen lost not only their homes but their nets and other tackle needed to carry on their work at sea - and the catch that they had brought home as the fire started, cooked on the quay. The peril that they faced was usually on the sea, but disaster had found them ashore, in their home port.

An appeal for funds was made in the area but so great was the devastation, beyond the possibility of redevelopment, that for the first time ever Southwold was declared a disaster area nationally and a nationwide appeal for donations was launched. But, even so, the devastated areas could only be left as greens.

In pre-fire insurance days, it was customary for Briefs, official appeals, to be made. The first insurance office, the Phoenix, opened in London in 1667, in the aftermath of the capital's Great Fire, but it was 1710 before another company, the Sun, began provincial cover. Both were far too late for Southwold. So, a Brief was prepared and issued giving details of the disaster and the losses suffered and authorising a collection to be made. It would be read out in parish churches during a service and money would be collected from the congregation as they left.

In Southwold's case, the Brief was addressed to the Bishop of Norwich and was read in churches in Norfolk and Suffolk with the appeal open until early June but, so great was the town's need that, as that Brief ended, a second, national Brief, to last a year, was authorised. It was to be read before the Nicene Creed in every church in the land, the first of its kind, beginning a practice that was to annoy Samuel Pepys. Southwold's may have been the first, but national Briefs grew so many that two years later, in his diary entry for 30 June 1661, Pepys complained that 'the trade in briefs is come now up to so constant a cause every Sunday that we resolve to give no more to them'.

In Newmarket, as in fires elsewhere, there was 'a very high winde'. It came over the Heath and into the town on the evening of Thursday, 22 March 1683. It found a flame in a stable yard in the area of St Mary's church, 'near the little stone bridge near the market place'. It is uncertain what caused the flame. Perhaps a torch, or the 'carelessness of a groom taking tobacco'.

The fire flew with the wind through the crowded jumble of poor properties, dwellings, stables, beer houses and inns in the more squalid part of the town, running behind and along the St Mary's side of the High Street towards the present Clock Tower and Bury Road, but it also consumed sixty-six 'mansion houses'. Attempts were made to save the many horses 'which were taken out of the Flame and let loose upon the Street, to shift for themselves with the People', but it did not prevent tragedy as they 'instead of making towards the Heath, made to the stables, where they were burnt without all possibility of preventing it'.

One side of Newmarket burned. The other side, the All Saints side, got the smoke, billows of the stuff foul with the stench of burning horses, stables and muck-heaps. In the middle of that smoke was King Charles II in his palace fronting onto the High Street.

Charles went to Newmarket several times a year taking a noble entourage with him and making the town, in effect, the capital of England. His palace was nothing grand. He had bought 'an old wretched house of my Lord Thomond's' and the *Greyhound Inn* next to it. As a modern developer might, he had had the two knocked together and extended. It apparently remained wretched, or so his close acquaintances thought, 'plac'd in a dirty streete', but Charles was happy enough. It served his purpose. Newmarket was a place he enjoyed, where he could be one of the local gentry rather than the king. And his time there was filled with pleasurable diversions, from end to end, and was never a bore. After the sobriety of Cromwell's rule there seemed an excess of gratification. He went hawking in the mornings, to the cockfighting in the afternoons, and to the races whenever they were on. In the evenings he could enjoy plays, gambling, the company of women or a drink amongst friends at one of the town's inns.

Charles was especially ready to enjoy his sojourn in Newmarket in the spring of 1683. He was getting older and his health was not as good as it had once been. Recently he had been ill with a fever and had almost died, creating a ferment of intrigue over who was to succeed him. That intrigue still continued while he was in Newmarket.

His legitimate heir was his brother, James, the Duke of York, and Charles would hear of no other successor despite the fact that James was a papist and highly unpopular. Charles would have liked to choose his illegitimate son, the Protestant Duke of Monmouth, but that was out of the question. He was not his heir, much as Monmouth himself wanted to be, and they had fallen out over it. That saddened Charles. He wanted to be on good terms with him but the boy, as sons often are, was very trying. He thought that the throne should go to him and that was the one thing that his father must deny him. Others thought Monmouth should be the next King of England, too. He had attracted a band of fanatics about him to support his claim and things had become unpleasant. Charles must have been glad to escape to the fresh air of Newmarket Heath, to the sports, the comfort of a woman, the company of friends.

And then suddenly, damn it, the fresh air was gone and his palace was full of stinking smoke. He couldn't see his hand in front of him, or the rings on his fingers. His eyes were stinging, and as for coughing . . .

He had planned to stay in Newmarket for a while longer. He was not ready to go back to London and the cares that he had left there. He would still stay. He left his palace, moving away from the smoke and the danger – the wind could change direction and spread the fire across the narrow High Street to his palace – and went to spend the night at Lord Suffolk's house.

He stayed on in Newmarket for another three or four days but, it was no good, the pleasure had gone. Some of the Lords with him, Sunderland, Clarendon, Clifford and Rochester, had lost their best horses in the fire and were being tiresome about it. And how could he enjoy half a town when many of his favourite diversions had been in the half that was reduced to ashes?

He decided, after all, to return to London earlier than he had originally intended, and that saved his life, frustrating the Rye House Plot. Supporters of Monmouth had planned to ambush his coach and assassinate him as he reached the mansion in Hoddesdon, Hertfordshire, but he was on the road before they were prepared and reached London safely, 'crown'd with Mercy', still the king of his realm, a good or a bad thing depending on allegiance.

At a meeting of the Suffolk Quarter Sessions, held in Bury St Edmunds, damages in Newmarket were estimated at £20,265.4s.8d (c.£1.7 million today). Many people suffered loss, but only three died. And there were some who had not suffered as much as they claimed. A couple of weeks after the fire an item in the *London Gazette* stated that, 'Whereas several idle Persons are wandering and begging from place to place, pretending to be undone by the late dreadful Fire at Newmarket, These are to give notice, That there is not one Person of the said Town abroad craving Relief.' Conmen were about even then!

What relief was needed by anyone in the town was to come from a Brief put out by the Lord Chancellor which, according to accounts, raised £20,000. But had it? Five years later, according to the *London Gazette* again, not a penny had been paid out 'to the great prejudice of the poor Sufferers by the Fire at Newmarket'. More conmen?

As early as 1567 Bungay had leather fire buckets, kept on pegs inside St Mary's church. They served their purpose in lesser fires from that time, but they were of little use in the two Great Fires to hit the town in 1652 and, most destructively, on Friday, 1 March 1688.

The fire that Friday began at dawn in an unoccupied tenement in the Market Place. Today, someone sleeping rough, or teenagers messing about, might be blamed. Then, while the fire spread to consume the town, suspicion fell on papists. Catholic James had succeeded his brother Charles in 1685, but in Protestant England he had proved too divisive to last long. In 1688 there had been the Glorious Revolution to remove James from the throne and, just two weeks before the Bungay fire, he had been replaced by the Protestant Dutchman, William of Orange, and his wife, Mary.

There were several prominent Catholics in the Bungay area and, in the atmosphere of the day, probably wrongly, they were thought responsible. It was just as likely to have been the ecumenical hand of God, neither Catholic not Protestant.

The fire speedily consumed Easham Street and then began a rampage. St Mary's church was in the heart of the fire, the heat so intense that the bells in the tower melted. It burned from the inside as well as the outside as people dragged smouldering belongings from their homes into the church for safety and set fire to the wooden benches. From there it spread to the roof, the tower, and to the steeple. Holy Trinity was also badly damaged but, perhaps having a less foolhardy congregation, it escaped the fate of St Mary's. Recorded in the churchwarden's book is, 'Paid Robert Dalby and three men for helping to quench ye fire at ye church and to carry the rubbish out. 4/-.' It had wisely been decided that it would be worth paying four shillings to have it quenched!

When the fire ended, six hours after it had begun, 190 dwellings had been lost as well as commercial premises, the staithe and the grammar school, and 900 people had lost either their home or their livelihood. But there was only one death.

It had been a dry spring in the substantial village of Debenham in 1744. At the beginning of March there was little water in the stream. And that was a bigger misfortune than anyone could have foretold. On 3 March every drop of water would be needed, but a river as broad and deep as any in the land would hardly have been enough.

Shortly after nine that morning a scream was heard and then a shout of 'Fire!' The village bakery, owned by widow Rosella Summers, who had been running the business alone since her husband's death, was burning.

As she stood, helpless and distraught, in the street, a crowd of spectators already gathering about her, men climbed ladders to pull down the blazing thatch while others ran to and fro with what water they could find, mainly at the church where the fire buckets were kept. But, even as the first buckets reached the bakery, it was too late. Fire was in the eaves and feeding on the oven-dried timbers.

The bakery stood alone. It was lost, reduced to smoking ashes, but at least the fire would not spread. Or would it? As on so many occasions of catastrophic fire, there was a wind, a lively March wind. It whirled through the glowing remains of the bakery breathing new life into the embers, lifting sparks to the thatched roofs of a row of cottages on the opposite side of the street. They burst into flame. All was dry and, apart from an occasional tiled roof, the fire had unobstructed passage from house to house all the way through Debenham.

The fire was still burning the next day. Farmers in nearby Pentaugh, Winston and Framsden sent men and teams of horses to help where they could, but they were as useless as the few buckets of water tossed into the inferno, as useless as the sightseers who were turning up in increasing numbers to gawp at devastation.

The third day, 5 March, the fire ended, not because it had been doused at last but because it had run out of things to burn.

After the fire, Debenham tried to raise the money to buy a fire engine, but all spare cash was needed to rebuild what had been lost. It was 1824 before a collection succeeded in raising enough money to buy a Shand Mason manual fire engine for £97. By 1835 they had another £83 and used that to build a fire station.

As it turned out, they had done the right thing. At about half past nine on the morning of Thursday, 20 September 1849 there was an explosion in a stable at Debenham's *Angel Inn*. No. Not a horse with flatulence. The stable, of timber and thatch and of an uncertain age, was being used to store fireworks in readiness for a celebration of the Anniversary of the Society of Oddfellows. Something, unknown, had set them off. Unlike a century before, the village's fire engine was soon on the scene, along with others from nearby Stonham and Thorndon. Villagers backed them up and the fire was quickly contained. There was no repeat of 1744.

Debenham Parish Council continued to fund its own fire engine through to the twentieth century, crewed by up to twenty volunteers, willing village men in flat caps, farm workers' garb and wellington boots. They were paid 2/- per practice and 5/- for drying the hose, but the real earner was attending a fire. If the fire lasted less than six hours each man got 7/6 plus 1/6 for refreshments - but that was docked if the person whose fire they were extinguishing put the kettle on and made them a mug of tea. For a fire lasting more than six hours, 1/- per hour per fireman was added.

Over a century after the Great Fire of Bungay, on Thursday, 4 May 1789, in a time of revolution, with the French soon to storm the Bastille and George Washington elected as the first president of a newly independent America, it was Brandon's turn to burn. Revolution could not have been farther from the thoughts of everyone in the Suffolk town, a small rural settlement but of national consequence for its production of gunflints and rabbit skins, when in mid-afternoon fire broke out in the home of the surgeon, Francis Henry Shanley, in Ferry Street, now the High Street, stretching from Market Hill to a bridge over the Little Ouse. Someone, most probably a servant or housekeeper, had thrown hot ashes out onto a muck heap. The muck heap was next to a wooden shed thatched with straw. It was a windy day which fanned the embers to ignite the straw. Everything went up in smoke, Shanley's wearing apparel, and there were fashionable, costly items amongst it, his wife's clothing, and all that the house contained, including drugs and medical equipment.

From Shanley's house the fire reached Elizabeth Cooper's tenement next door. Some houses, by then, were being made of brick, but that did not prevent some newly-built ones being destroyed. The occupants of one of them, the postmaster, William Webb, and his wife, narrowly escaped with their lives, as did their neighbours. Their lives were all that they did save.

The fire sped on, hastened by a south-westerly wind. It jumped to the opposite side of the street where it demolished dwellings, some of which had barns, stables and brewhouses attached, and the premises of a whitesmith, a blacksmith, a saddler, a brewer and two tailors. All contents were lost except that one of the tailors, George Warner, managed to save his bed. He shared premises with the man who lost most in the fire, saddler Francis Diggon, who was also a fellmonger, a dealer in animal skins. Together they lost personal effects and goods of their trades amounting to something in the region of £700 when most had lost less than £10. But Diggon could have fared worse. His cash in coin was later recovered from the ashes.

By cruel fate – and fate often was cruel in those days of the great town fires – Brandon was a town, or large village, mostly of women when the disaster struck. It was a fair day in Thetford, a few miles away over the county boundary into Norfolk, and the younger men of Brandon, the ones who would fight fire, were at the fair. Still, there was a plentiful supply of water from the river and there were some men left who were active enough to set to work. Although of only about 200 houses, Brandon had a fire engine. Lord Montrath sent another from his estate at nearby Weeting Hall, and with great effort and determination the destruction of the whole community was prevented. And fate had not been entirely cruel. The wind that had spread the flames also stopped them, driving them away from more premises and towards the river. When the elsewhere fairgoers returned it was to the embers of some of their homes – and toast for tea.

Losses were great and, with the reticence of the time, only two victims had been insured, Francis Diggon being one of them. Relief of the sufferers was needed and within two weeks a committee of local gentlemen had formed to organise it. Briefs, as at Newmarket, were still the norm and in general use, but they were expensive to organise and often it would be four or five years, if then, before proceeds reached the needy. Once it had been determined that the Brandon fire had been accidental it was decided that an appeal should be made directly to the neighbourhood and it was underway in six or seven weeks, the Earl of Orford starting it off with a donation of £50 and saying that he would petition the local nobility and gentry. Lord Montrath gave £50.

Despite the usual scoundrels being about, going from house to house begging, claiming to be victims, the appeal was a success, although if the area's farmers and landowners had not had to bear losses of their own in a bad summer it may have been even more successful. Many individuals and almost every town and village around Brandon gave what they could. In all, 1,400 gave amounts from 2d upwards. Bury St Edmunds gave over £42. Local charity in action, and in little over a year all victims had received compensation. Mary Cooper, a servant who had lost her all, three gowns worth a few shillings, a pair of shoes and a repaired coat, would, at last, be able to deck herself anew, and far sooner than if the town had opted for a Brief.

Only gradually did improvements in fire prevention reach the provinces from London, and even more gradually did the provincial towns of Suffolk begin to take notice. When there was timber at hand, and reed and straw in plenty, ready to be cut – why not use them to build? The dangers of thatch were well known but roofing tiles or slates would have to be bought and brought in. They would be expensive, and not everywhere was as affluent as Bury St Edmunds with money to burn. Only slowly was it accepted that whatever the cost it would be less than that of another fire. The age of the Great Fire had run its course.

So, thatch was out at last, and, as long as everyone took care of their hearth and their candle, every town in Suffolk was a safer place. The few thatched properties that survive today are considered picturesque and olde worlde, reminders of an idyllic time gone by, the rampaging fires that they caused long forgotten. To renew a thatched roof now is the work of a skilled craftsman, the master of an almost obsolete art, and can cost tens of thousands of pounds. But, once done, well – it will last for donkey's years, wont it? Unless it goes up in flames. And they still do.

Chapter 4

Simple Pleasures

Communal entertainments were simple pleasures in the seventeenth and early eighteenth centuries. They did not happen very often and they had to be wholeheartedly enjoyed when they did – except, of course, in Cromwell's time when he banned everything that might encourage the people to forget their worries for a golden moment or two.

He abolished May Day, 1 May, a traditional annual holiday, but at one place at least, Bury St Edmunds in 1648, the people decided that they would rather fight than give up their day of enjoyment. About 600 people got together in the town and put up a maypole, daringly announcing that they had done so 'For God and King Charles!' They raided a weapons and ammunition store and made ready, in various positions about the streets, to defend themselves. They knew that they would have to. Perhaps that was an entertainment in itself.

When Colonel Whalley and his troops arrived to restore order there was a brief set-to in which two townsmen and two horses were killed, and then local MPs, Sir William Barnardiston and Sir William Playters, offered the rebels a pardon for their 'tumult' if they would give up their arms and behave themselves. They accepted.

The townspeople of Bury also revelled in their annual Autumn Fair, which had been held in the second week of October for 600 years. In 1818, and again in 1825, Madame Marie Tussaud brought her travelling exhibition to the fair. A great attraction was her 'Separate Room', a forerunner of the Chamber of Horrors when she established herself in a permanent site in London's Baker Street. It cost an extra sixpence to go in but it was well worth it to see the last remnants of a continental disaster, casts of the heads of the aristocrats guillotined in the French Revolution. With them were models of notorious criminals, with representations of their gory crimes, and instruments of torture unimagined in rural Suffolk.

But gradually, through the nineteenth century, the Bury fair became more of a nuisance than a pleasure with fairgoers preferring drinking, fighting and rowdiness to a swing boat ride and a piece of gingerbread. Daniel Defoe, in his travels throughout East Anglia in the 1720s, claimed that prostitutes plied their trade at the fair, a comedown from its former more respectable reputation as a marriage market, and by the 1870s it was so rife with crime and disorder that it faced abolition.

Everywhere entertainments drew the crowds, keen for diversion, but sometimes novelty went to their heads and they behaved like fools, with an abandon that could be deadly. In Lowestoft, in 1894, swing boats were still a popular ride when a young hand on one of the town's fishing boats paid his penny for a ride at the December Fair in the Market Place. With the ride at its height, swinging like a pendulum, he stood up to change places with a friend, lost his hold, fell about 16ft to the ground and died the next day in hospital.

In Walsham-le-Willows, north of Bury St Edmunds, in July 1911, it was at an annual gala that an argument over change given for a ride on the steam horses led to the villagers attacking the ride. Men working with the fair shot at them with rifles from the shooting gallery. The villagers, like most countrymen of the day, had rifles, and no fairground weapons for them, they were the real thing, and they went home to get them. A serious shoot-out began in which seven men were shot and the landlord of a nearby public house was killed as he drove innocently past the fair in his pony and trap.

But for holy disturbance little could beat the Ranters. In February 1823 120 Ranters, Primitive Methodists, crowded into a small room in the *City of Norwich* public house in St Stephen's Street in the city. The floor gave way under their weight throwing them 9ft down into the cellar below where they were 'with considerable difficulty extricated'. Twenty-five people, some of them children, were seriously injured. Several sustained fractures and one of them, a Great Yarmouth man, had such a bad fracture of his leg that it was amputated on the spot.

Primitive Methodists at that time seemed to have quite a reputation for excess. At Burwell in 1863 'the Primitive Methodists, commonly called Ranters, held a camp meeting in North Street on Sunday evening last. Like most meetings of this nature, we regret to learn that it ended in a sad scene of drunkenness and disorder'.

But Faith Teas, held on Good Fridays, were usually polite – if faith had provided enough food for everyone – and Burwell Feast, held at Pound Hill each Whitsuntide, was enjoyed by the whole neighbourhood.

It was a fair lasting a week, with crowds lively but good-natured – none of what went on down south at Walsham-le-Willows for them as they tried the rides and amusements. Swing boats were sure to be there. Perhaps there would be a troupe of acrobats. And there was usually a dancing booth. Simple pleasures.

The villagers of Burwell, like those throughout the area, had little to divert them from their sometimes samey rural lives beyond a church or chapel social of some kind, swimming in the Cam as it flowed by on its way to join the Great Ouse and go on to Ely, and their Feast. If a travelling entertainment arrived in the village, whatever it was, it was an excitement, an all-too-rare treat not to be missed.

One turned up unexpectedly on Friday, 8 September 1727. A puppeteer with his wife, daughter and servant came riding into the village, passing through on their way to Stourbridge Fair, twelve miles away on the north bank of the Cam in Cambridge. Always on the lookout for an opportunity to make money, Robert Shepherd, who was also something of a magician and expert in the sort of tricks where the speed of the hand deceives the eye, decided to delay going on to Stourbridge to put on a performance in Burwell.

As early as 1211 King John had granted Stourbridge Fair to the Leper Hospital at Barnwell in Cambridge but, with the dissolution of the hospital, it had been given to Cambridge Corporation. It had the rents and tolls while the university governed weights and measures and the licensing of shows, such as Shepherd's.

The Fair was erected on half a square mile of cleared cornfields between the present Newmarket Road, where the chapel of the Leper Hospital still stands, and the Cam, row upon row of booths dealing in virtually all the commodities of Britain and Europe. Defoe, in 1723, just four years before Shepherd planned to perform there, said that it was the greatest fair in the world.

It ran for three weeks in September, from St Bartholemew's Day, 7 September, to Michaelmas Day, after the corn harvest and before autumn ploughing, and was, as one writer has put it, 'like a well-governed city, and less disorder and confusion to be seen there than in any other place where there is so great a concourse of people'. It had its own peacekeeping force and a court of justice to try offenders, so it should have been orderly!

Trading, buyers and sellers coming from as far away as Italy, Spain, France and Germany as well as all parts of the British Isles, was retail and wholesale with, in the first days of the Fair, prodigious amounts of business being done, especially in wool, hops and leather. Anything and everything could be bought there, which was just as well for British science. It was at Stourbridge that Sir Isaac Newton bought the prisms – three for £3 and probably from Italy – used in his work to establish some of the first laws of physics.

After the serious wholesale business, the horse fair was held, and two or three days after that the many diversions and entertainments began. Local people, families, would flock there and, 'besides what is flung away to see the puppet shows, drolls, rope-dancing, live creatures etc., of which there is commonly plenty,' would spend money on fripperies, trinkets, toys and food and drink.

So, when Robert Shepherd reached Burwell on 8 September the Fair had only just begun and it would be a few days before he could expect to start performing there. He was early. A show on the way and some pennies coming in – why not? Perhaps his wife, Martha, and his daughter, also Martha, about ten-years-old, would rather have gone straight to the Fair to see more goods from more places than they had in their lives, but money was money, and there was time.

Shepherd rented a small barn, Wasson's or Wusson's Barn, in Cockles or Cuckolds Row, not far from the parish church of St Mary the Virgin, and the word was quickly spread. A magic and puppet show. That evening. Admission one penny.

It was an old barn with sturdy walls of clunch and mortar reaching 9ft up to a thatched roof which was shared by an adjoining stable, separated from the barn by a lath and plaster partition. The barn was 45ft long and about 17ft wide and was almost full of oat straw 'bound up in trusses'.

A space on the side closest to the stable was cleared for Shepherd's curtained booth, the trusses were stacked against the walls as high as the thatch, the excited audience rolled up and the pennies rolled in.

The whole of Burwell and the area for miles around was agog. It had been a long time since Whitsun and the pleasures of the Feast and everyone, the children and young people especially, were more than ready to see a show.

Far more people than could possibly fit in turned up with their penny admission, but about 140 were squeezed into a space little more than 4 yards by 4 yards. The barn was packed and still more people clamoured to get in. A few of them got annoyed at not being able to see the performance so, to be sure no one would try to force a way in, the door was locked, 'fast hasped by an iron staple', possibly by the puppet master himself.

To begin the show Shepherd did some tricks, some sleight of hand, to amaze the rustics, performing them on an oval wooden table with his audience crowding close to try to catch him out. A hidden card. A palmed penny. No chance. He bamboozled them all.

When that part of the show was finished the table was moved to the back of the barn, out of the way. Its raised ends were lowered and it was pushed flat against the locked door.

It was nine o'clock before the puppet show began, an autumn twilight falling along the village streets and over the surrounding fenland, lanterns being lit. And there were lanterns and candles lit in the barn, the brightest lighting the stage where the puppets began to act out their play to a delighted audience, children to the front so as not to miss a moment.

People were still outside the door and one young man in particular was annoyed at being kept out. He had been sure that he would be allowed in, and without paying, because he was employed by the owner of the barn and the stable next door. Richard Whitaker, from Hadstock, near Linton, was an ostler in his mid-twenties. He had put the puppeteer's two horses in the stable, had fed and watered them, settled them in, and then he had been ready to watch the show. He was an employee, he was part of the whole thing, and there should have been a place for him, without a penny, but there he was outside the door.

Exasperated, he went back into the stable, with his lighted candle, and climbed up to the hayloft. From beneath the thatch he could hear the performance and, moving on to the tops of the trusses, he could see the puppet booth against the partition. Along the space, above the barn, he could see someone else, a lad, who had done the same. He was sitting on a beam, his candle beside him, looking down at the puppets. He was sixteen-year-old Thomas Howe.

What happened next is unclear. It was so at the time – eyewitnesses to a disaster today rarely agree on all the details of what took place – and it has remained so.

One version says that a boy 'climbed up upon some beams and took his candle with him' and 'while he was viewing ye show fell down amongst a heap of straw and find it alight which ye boy perceiving he sprang out and narrowly escaped'. Had that been Thomas Howe?

Thomas Howe, returning to the scene with Reverend Thomas Gibbons some years later told him that, from his seat in the barn, he had been able to look across the straw into the hayloft and saw the fire 'when it was so small as that he thinks he could have inclosed it in his hands'. Had he looked to where Richard Whitaker was concealed?

There may have been a whiff of smoke at that stage. If so, no one paid attention. It would be candle smoke. And then fire 'like lightning' flew round the barn in an instant.

It had been a hot, dry summer. There had been a drought. Everything, hay, straw and thatch, was dry. From the roof, fire shot down the trusses against the walls and across the straw scatterings on the floor. Everyone in the barn, in a matter of moments, was in a box of fire and, in panic and terror, rushed for the door.

The door was locked. Gibbons, in his booklet *An Account of a Most Terrible FIRE, Etc*, published in 1769, forty-two years after the disaster, says that the door was 'so narrow as that it was only three feet in breadth, including the posts', and that it opened inwards. Whether it did or not was of no consequence when it was secured. It was usual for barns to have a door large enough to allow a loaded cart to enter. It is possible that the door Gibbons refers to was let into the larger one for a person to use. If so, it was not meant for the use of 140 burning people fighting to get out through 'the only way of deliverance from the tremendous destruction'.

Frenzied commotion. Shepherd looked out from behind the curtains of his puppet booth. Fire, all around. He called to his wife, 'Martha, we shall certainly be burnt!' The show was over.

Everyone rushed to the door, falling over each other, being trampled down, engulfed in smoke and flame, the flame through the thatch setting light to adjacent properties where one old, bedridden woman, Mary Woodbridge, died. Borne on a strong, dry wind, burning straw was carried 300 yards to set fire to another barn.

The alarm spread so quickly that almost at once the rest of Burwell knew that a great tragedy was taking place. It was a close-knit community of about 800 families, with most villagers knowing of someone, kin or friend, in the barn that night.

But it was a visitor to Burwell, Thomas Dobedee from the village of Wicken, 3 or 4 miles away across the fen, who took action. He was 'a very stout man in the prime of life' and he managed to break down the door and then to drag some people out. Again and again, helped by two other men, he saved whoever he could until he was 'in danger of being destroyed himself, the very hair of his head having been singed by the flames'.

When the door was forced open young Thomas Howe, as he retold it, jumped down from his beam onto the mass of people below, bodies lying three and four deep, and 'he sprang out at the upper part of the opening made by the breaking of the door, and was not in the least injured by the fire'. He was fortunate, as were a few other people who managed to escape by climbing over bodies to reach the door.

All that had happened in a very short time. The inferno had been instant. After about half an hour 'down descended the thatch of a roof seventeen feet and a half in height, no doubt in the fiercest blaze, upon the helpless hopeless creatures, and not improbably the trusses of straw, when their bands were burnt, rolled down upon them in so many volumes of flame, and thus one ruin was heaped upon another'.

Gibbons could not bring himself to describe the horror of the remains found at dawn the next morning. An 1884 version of a 1727 manuscript is less caring about 'the tender reader'. It pulls no punches. 'After the fire was abated they found here an arm and there a leg, here a head, there a body, some burnt with their bowels hanging out, most deplorable sight.'

Most were burned beyond identification and the remains were just shovelled into carts and taken to the churchyard where two mass graves had been hastily prepared. Dead was every female who had attended the show, and fifty-one children died. Two children of the Palmer family, John and Ann, were the only recognisable victims and were buried separately. Their mother was not. Two people died a day or so later, one of them Robert Shepherd's servant.

The mass graves spared the vicar of St Mary's, Reverend Alexander Edmondson, the necessity of conducting a separate funeral for each victim. He held one service and preached one sermon. His text, from Lamentations, was painfully appropriate: 'Their visage is blacker than a coal; they are not known in the streets; their skin cleaveth to their bones; it is withered, it is become like a stick.'

The finger of blame pointed at Richard Whitaker. He was arrested and, six months later, on 27 March 1728, he was tried at Cambridge Assizes, but he was a young man of good character and, against the opinion of many people in Burwell, the jury acquitted him of negligence and arson for lack of evidence.

Eighty-one people in all died, including the puppeteer and his family, and all for a pennyworth of entertainment, a simple pleasure. In Burwell, amid modern housing, a plaque marks the probable site of Wasson's Barn. In St Mary's churchyard there is a simple headstone carved with a heart in flames.

Chapter 5

Wreck

In the Great Gale of 1692 200 ships and over 1,000 lives were lost in just one night in the treacherous waters off the Norfolk coast, in the same place where, a little over twenty years before, in September 1671, a storm had wrecked seventy-five vessels. It was said that 'the sea is so full of wreck on these coasts that those at sea are forced to look out sharp to steer clear of it.'

And that was what the East Anglian coast was about. North Sea storms were frequent and ferocious, wrecking, shifting the numerous foundering sandbanks as they raged. In winter especially the prevailing off-shore westerly wind would become a north-easterly, thrashing down from Scandinavia and the Arctic, battering an exposed lee shore. Ships which managed to sail a safe course through elusive sands would risk being smashed by the force of the waves, overwhelmed, or driven ashore.

Merchant ships, coasters, colliers and fishing vessels sailed East Anglian waters and, in the days of sail, the sea lanes were busier than a Bank Holiday motorway. A storm created a havoc of torn canvas, tangled ropes, splintered masts, timbers and dead bodies. Entire fishing fleets could be lost. Every boat and every man. In 1789, around 130 fishing smacks and coasters were wrecked between Southwold and Cromer.

Great Yarmouth, it used to be said, was 'raised from the waters and built on the bones of herring'. For two centuries Yarmouth *was* herrings, but the price was high in boats and men. In February 1877, when a gale hit the fishing fleet, forty smacks were sunk without trace and 100 men did not return home. But as many, and more, Yarmouth men took their places. Into the twentieth century well over 1,000 vessels sailed out of the port landing, in 1913, the peak of the herring trade, 213 cran, a cran being 28 stone.

With so many thousands of vessels, so many storms, the losses over the years are beyond number, and in the churchyards of the coastal churches, where the vicars would shine a saving light from their towers to warn seafarers of danger, are the graves and memorials of those who did not come safely home to port.

Britain prided herself on having the greatest navy in the world, her sea battles renowned and her admirals the nation's heroes. Horatio Nelson was a Norfolk man and all of East Anglia claimed him. But still East Anglian seas were a challenge to every Royal Navy ship, just as they were to the smallest rowboat afloat. Here is the fate of some of them.

On 19 December 1770 a severe storm hit the region, blowing down trees and blocking roads. At Norwich, part of the city wall was blown down. The storm lashed Norfolk, destroying buildings, smashing churches and overturning windmills. At sea the whole coast, Happisburgh, Sea Palling, Caister, was strung with wrecks.

The storm continued into the next day when the eight-gun Royal Navy sloop, HMS *Peggy*, found herself gripped in a snow-laden gale that was driving her towards shore. The *Peggy*, although often used in the control of smuggling, a thriving occupation in the North Sea, was returning from other duties. News had reached Britain that Spain had occupied the Falkland Islands and war seemed inevitable. Impressment warrants had been sent to Newcastle and the Peggy and HMS *Little Dick*, a brig, had been ordered there to serve as reception vessels for pressed men.

There was always a shortage of skilled seamen in wartime, only naval officers were career men and, since the 1560s, the practice was to force 'eligible men of seafaring habits' into the service. It was unpopular, it was resisted by the coastal towns whenever a press gang turned up, but, in the name of the Sovereign, it was legal. In particular, they wanted merchant seamen already familiar with ships and the sea and a good quantity had been found in Newcastle.

On Tuesday, 18 December, the day before the storm, both vessels had set sail down the east coast, bound for the Nore. By noon on the Wednesday, as the storm was about to begin, they were 4 miles off Cromer. Both vessels continued along the coast but, with darkness, the wind strengthened to gale force and the *Peggy* lost her trysail mast. At 6pm the pilot advised that both vessels should anchor, but the *Little Dick* could not be seen in the deteriorating visibility.

In the early hours of Thursday morning, as Lieutenant George Robertson went on watch, there was a sudden change in the wind, it swung to NNE, its most dangerous quarter, and the snow-lashed shore of

Happisburgh loomed ever closer as she was blown helplessly towards it.

Captain Richard Toby ordered all heavy casks of water and beer to be thrown overboard to lighten the *Peggy*. The main mast was cut away and the sheet anchor was let go. They were all the right things to do, but they were not enough to save her. She went aground at Happisburgh Town Gap at 7am with waves crashing over her decks.

It was five hours later, into the afternoon, before the tide and the wind eased enough for Happisburgh villagers, led by John Shepheard, bailiff of the manor, to take wagons to the vessel and carry fifty-nine surviving crew and pressed men to safety. Many, including Toby, were utterly exhausted, but Robertson, young and vigorous, was able to help with the rescue and the bringing ashore of the dead, and later with the saving of the ship's stores.

The *Little Dick*, more fortunate than the *Peggy*, although she lost her fore topsail and staysail, reached Yarmouth, but she immediately received orders to return to the scene of the disaster and pick up the fifty-nine survivors. Amongst them were fourteen pressed men who were not keen to continue their naval service. Within hours of its starting they had been in a severe storm, had been shipwrecked and had narrowly escaped death and they wanted to go home. They refused to board the *Little Dick*. As Captain Toby reported: 'the new raised men who remained on the spot, appeared armed with clubs, and refused to go on board the tender, on which myself and the Lieutenant used every means of inducing them to go on board, however they deserted.' The penalties for desertion were severe but Toby had no option but to let them go – back to Newcastle.

Thirty-two men on the *Peggy* lost their lives. They were buried in Happisburgh churchyard. The wreck of the *Peggy*, half buried in the sand, remained on the beach for many years, a reminder that, as the Court Martial determined, her crew 'did their utmost to preserve the said sloop and the loss was unavoidably occasioned by the badness of the weather'.

And Captain Toby had generous praise for Lieutenant Robertson. 'Most of those who survived from the *Peggy* owe their preservation to that gentleman, who being blessed with uncommonly strong constitution retained his strength and senses when myself and most of the crew were deprived thereof, and he exerted himself in a most extraordinary manner.' In consequence, he was given command of a cutter, the *Prince George*.

In Nelson's time, the great ships of the line must have been breathtaking to see. Even the seventy-four gun Ramilles class HMS *Invincible*, thirty-six years old in the spring of 1801 and battle-wearied, was a stirring sight, fully rigged.

Launched at Deptford in March 1765, the *Invincible* had served in the American War of Independence. Her battle honours included Cape St Vincent 1780, Chesapeake 1781, St Kitts 1782 and the Glorious First of June 1794. In 1797 she had played a part in the capture of Trinidad from the Spanish. In March 1801, after so many years of valiant service in distant seas, she was in British waters.

From Chatham, she sailed to Yarmouth, where she called for orders before continuing on her way to join the Baltic Fleet under Admiral Sir Hyde Parker and his second-in-command, Admiral Horatio Nelson, for the Battle of Copenhagen.

Denmark had long used its neutrality in Europe for its merchants to profit by transporting goods for warring powers. In 1801, several European ports were being blockaded by France but Denmark had entered a Napoleon-inspired neutrality pact and was still trading. Britain determined to smash the pact to gain access to the Baltic. The Battle of Copenhagen, the one where Nelson refused to obey an order to withdraw by holding his telescope to his blind eye, resulted in victory for Britain. But not for *Invincible*.

The first appointment of thirty-four-year-old Captain John Rennie, the 1,631 tons burthen vessel was fully loaded with all provisions and ordnance necessary to service her crew of 600 men in a war situation. She was as prepared as she could be for the battle ahead.

With Rear Admiral of the Blue Thomas Totty on board and flying his flag, she sailed from Yarmouth on the morning of Monday, 16 March. Because of the known dangers of the seas off Norfolk, especially the sandbanks, she had a pilot and master on board to guide her through the Haisboro Gap.

Early in the afternoon, with a strong tide running, the wind freshened and she was forced off course. At two-thirty she struck a sandbank, Hammond's Knoll, east of Haisboro Sands. For several hours efforts were made to float her free, and her guns repeatedly fired a distress signal, but, when the mizzen mast went and she was still stuck fast, the main mast was cut away. After an all-night struggle, during which her cargo was jettisoned, she found deeper water but, as she did so, in a heavy swell and freshening wind, she lost her rudder. Unmanageable, she was driven back onto the sandbank.

The *Invincible*'s distress signals had been answered by the revenue cutter *Hunter*, but she did not come to her aid. She ignored her plight. It was the Yarmouth smack *The Nancy*, fishing for cod under her skipper, Daniel Grigson, which did.

By then, after midnight, it was accepted that the *Invincible* was lost. Two of her boats were lowered. With Totty, the purser, four young midshipmen and some seamen in one, and seamen in the other, they safely reached *The Nancy*. The boats made a second run, but one capsized as it neared *The Nancy* and the lives of the men thrown into the sea were saved by a collier which had also answered *Invincible*'s distress signal. She stayed to save more of the crew.

Both rescue vessels remained at anchor through that Monday night although unable to be of any help to *Invincible* herself. Those on board could only watch the death throes of a great old ship-of-war as she drifted once more into deeper water and slowly sank, taking with her 400 men.

As she went down, seventy men on the forecastle made a last desperate attempt to get on board the *Invincible*'s launch. She became overcrowded, but still more scrambled to board her, threatening a capsize. Mercilessly, to save those already on her, they were beaten back by the oars.

A total of 196 were saved from the ship which, in addition to its crew of 600, had been carrying, somewhat bizarrely considering that it was going to war, fifty passengers. Young Captain Rennie was amongst the dead. The last to leave his ship, he had tried to swim to the launch, and he had almost made it. When within reach of the oars, overcome by cold and exhaustion, 'he lifted his hands to the sky, placed them over his face, and sank calmly beneath the waves'. Totty, reporting his loss, called him 'a truly zealous and intelligent Officer.'

At Sheerness, a fortnight after the *Invincible* went down, a court martial was held aboard HMS *Ruby* to try the survivors for the loss of their ship. Blame fell on the pilot and the master, both deceased. From Yarmouth Roads, under their guidance, *Invincible* had been steering with a free wind and, until thirty minutes before she struck the sandbank, land had been in sight to give them their bearings. When she grounded, both men said that the bank was new, made or reshaped by recent bad weather, but in court it was proved that there had been nothing new about it. She had hit the long-established Hammond's Knoll, exactly where it was known to be. They had not allowed for the rapidity of the tide. Both men, gone down with the ship and not present to defend themselves, were found guilty. Totty, the officers, and all the men who had survived, were found not guilty. Their conduct was said to have been 'highly meritorious'.

Over the days following the sinking, when, after the Battle of Copenhagen, Nelson visited the injured, 'his men', in a Yarmouth hospital, bodies were washed up all along the coast. At Happisburgh, they were collected by the cartload and taken up to the churchyard to join the men from HMS *Peggy*. A mass grave was dug for 119 of them, a grass mound their only memorial until, in 1913, a Happisburgh villager, Mary Cator, decided that there should be some reminder of the lives lost. She started a county-wide collection to raise funds for a stone, a plain granite cross, but, when it was found, following correspondence in the *Eastern Daily Press*, that there was no written record proving that the men were buried beneath the mound, she was compelled to return all donations and the grave stayed unmarked. But Mrs Cator remained determined. In 1924, when the St Mary's bells were rehung, she gave a treble bell bearing the inscription 'In memory of Nelson's men wrecked off Haisboro in 1801.' A memorial of a kind, at last, but it was not to be all.

In 1988, when a drainage trench was dug close to the mound, skeletons, and many of them, were found. That was taken as proof that the burial had indeed taken place and, in July 1998, a memorial service was held by the mound attended by members of the Nelson Society, officers, men and women of the Royal Navy, and a descendant of Captain John Rennie. A stone given jointly by the present HMS *Invincible*, an aircraft carrier, and the Parochial Church Council, a rectangular slab rather than a granite cross, was dedicated. The memorial, the rector Reverend Doctor Richard Hines, said, could be 'interpreted as a gesture of Christian faith that even in their most desperate moments those who perished out in that cold North Sea did not perish beyond the love and presence of Almighty God'. The inscription, from Revelation, reads: 'And the sea gave up the dead that were in it.'

The Yarmouth-based revenue cutter, *Hunter*, chose not to respond to the distress signals of the sinking *Invincible*. Had she done so, many lives may have been saved. She left salvation to the more willing but less able smack and an unwieldy collier brig and sailed off, not into the sunset, but to meet her own nemesis.

In a north-easterly gale on the night of 18 February 1807, the *Hunter* was driven into shallow water, her stern to the cliffs off Winterton, just north of the Cart Gap. In her wreck, her commander, Captain T Jay, and all her crew, died. In Happisburgh churchyard their bodies joined those of the men whose call for help they had ignored six years before. Perhaps, generously, the newcomers were welcomed home and allowed, later, to share their memorial.

Smuggling was rife all along the East Anglian coast and the revenue men, on land and at sea, were always given more than enough to do seizing illicit goods and those involved in their traffic, many of them local seafarers.

After the wreck of the *Hunter*, a new revenue cutter, the *Ranger*, took her place along the Norfolk coast. She quickly earned a reputation for her merciless pursuit of offenders. The feelings that she aroused in all who lived by and on the sea she patrolled bordered on hatred. Local sympathies were always with the smugglers.

So, when the *Ranger*, in her turn, was caught in a storm on 30 October 1822 and driven ashore, not far from where the *Hunter* had been wrecked, none of the inhabitants of Happisburgh heard the cries of those on board and there was no response to her signals for help even though she was within sight and sound of men ashore.

The cutter, along with Captain John Sayers and forty of his men, was lost and accusations soon began in the *Norfolk Chronicle* that 'by the shameful neglect of the inhabitants of Happisburgh neither boat nor Captain Manby's apparatus was got to the spot' even though 'the shrieks of the unfortunate men were heard distinctly on the shore'. George Manby, Master of the Great Yarmouth Artillery in the early eighteenth century and an inventor of devices for saving lives from shipwrecked vessels had made a line-throwing mortar, a forerunner of the modern rocket, approved by the Admiralty in 1808. It had been used with success from that year.

That provoked outrage and a furious response from those accused in the next edition of the paper. They had, they said, already rescued eighteen fishing boats and their crews in the storm before the *Ranger* was wrecked. And they had got out Manby's gun, but the distance had been too far for it to be used. It had been a serious gale with numerous vessels caught up in it and wrecked. The beach at Yarmouth, 'and for many miles', was 'covered in pieces of wrecks and bodies washed ashore'. At Happisburgh, they had gone to the aid of wreck after wreck in a matter of hours along a shore that was infamous for being a vessels' graveyard, so, to be fair, let it be said that they had more than done their duty. It was just unfortunate, they said, that the nineteenth wreck of the night happened to be a revenue cutter. Today, it can only be accepted as the truth. By the end of the nineteenth century their beach had become so strewn with wrecks that Trinity House used explosives to clear it.

It was a few miles north of Happisburgh, at Wells-next-the Sea, that there was a disaster just off shore in 1879. In the foulest of weather on 22 February the torpedo boat, HMS *Alarm*, made a routine voyage to take supplies to the coastguard station at Wells. On that occasion the main item being taken was a Morse signalling lamp.

The *Alarm* used its own lamp to signal to the Wells coastguards that they would have to come out to the vessel to collect it. Chief Boatman John Devlin signalled back that the weather was too bad. They only had a four-man rowing boat, a gig. But the *Alarm* would have none of it. She had brought the lamp and it must be fetched.

So the little boat set off, rowed by four coastguards and with Devlin at the helm. They rowed for two hours against the wind, but when they rounded a point it became impossible to stay on course. Another of the Wells coastguards, Williams, went to the point to signal to the *Alarm* that the boat was on its way, but what he saw was the boat capsized about 20 yards from the shore and Devlin clinging to it. There was no sign of the other four men – Perry, Bearman, Jordan and Driscoll.

Williams sent a signal to the quay at Wells, a mile away, and then he plunged into the freezing water to drag the boat, with Devlin still clinging to it, to safety. He barely survived the ordeal. Devlin did not. He died a few hours later as searchers scoured the area for his four colleagues. The bodies of Bearman and Jordan were found. A further search the next morning found Perry and Driscoll – and more besides. Searchers also found a wrecked rowing boat from HMS *Alarm*, but all who had been on board her were lost.

Whoever it had been on the *Alarm* issuing the orders that had sent five coastguards to their deaths had, it seemed, grown so impatient waiting for them to reach him that he had sent the six-man boat from the *Alarm* to take the Morse lamp to them. All that was ever revealed was that it had not been the captain. He had not known that the boat and six of his men had left his vessel until a signal from shore told him of the tragedy.

That came out at the inquest when a verdict of accidental death was returned into the needless deaths of eleven men. The jury asked the coroner to say, on their behalf, that 'they didn't think any fisherman well-acquainted with the coast would have put to sea in such weather as the Coastguardsmen did' and 'when the wind blows from a northerly direction the flood makes with great rapidity and a very dangerous current runs in the channel and breakers of tremendous force roll over the sandbank beyond the Point'.

The Wells coastguards, all married men in their thirties and forties, left five women widows and seventeen children fatherless – and all for the sake of a Morse lamp.

Countless disasters, the wrecks of vessels and lives, have marked the East Anglian coast. Today, in an era of sophisticated navigational aids, the off-shore seas are much safer, but nothing can eliminate all danger. There will always be human error, human frailty and the weather.

And a last few words. They could fit nowhere else but at the end. All wrecks are disasters but one, at least, had a lighter side. No lives were lost, only reputations, and even the goat was saved. On 1 January 1799 a 38-gun frigate, HMS *Apollo*, commanded by Captain Halkett, arrived in Yarmouth with some of her crew hurt. About thirty of them had been knocked down and injured in an accident with a capstan as the anchor was being weighed.

The *Apollo* sailed again on 5 January, short of complement, to cruise the North Sea towards the Dutch coast, but, in bad weather early in the morning of 7 January, she ran aground on the Haak sandbank, and it seemed to those aboard that she would stay there. It was late in the afternoon when a small Prussian galliot came to her aid and the decision was made to abandon the *Apollo*. To make room for her crew of 250, some of the galliot's cargo was thrown overboard, but only some – and its cargo was wine.

The galliot only had enough water for its own crew so the officers from the *Apollo*, twenty-two of them jammed into a small cabin, and the more than 200 men in the hold with the cargo, were required to drink wine during the three days and nights that it took to return them to Yarmouth. And they were thirsty men. They were more than very happy by the time they got to Yarmouth, but they quickly sobered up when the captain of a cutter belonging to the *Apollo* arrived to say that he had gone on board her after she had been abandoned and had found her in perfect shipshape order, floating like a duck. He had walked about her, collected his clothes from his wardrobe, and the ship's goat from the deck, and had left her as he had found her, safe and sound. They were in trouble.

Aboard the 64-gun HMS *Monmouth* at Yarmouth on 15 January, Captain Halkett and all of his officers and crew were tried by court martial for the loss of the *Apollo*. It could be that the humour of the situation was appreciated because they were all acquitted. Perhaps they had a drink – to celebrate their escape from a disgraceful end to their Royal Navy careers.

Chapter 6

The Yarmouth Catastrophe

In 1848, Charles Dickens stayed at the *Royal Hotel* on Yarmouth seafront, soaking up the atmosphere of the bustling maritime resort before writing *David Copperfield*. Many of today's visitors see Great Yarmouth perhaps as Dickens did, a stretch of fine sandy beach, where some of the action in the book took place. But now it is full of amenities, with entertainments and amusements constantly on tap for holidaymakers to enjoy.

Most do not look long at the other face of Yarmouth, the commercial quayside, where merchant ships and ferries dock and supply boats go to and from the off-shore rigs, and the rivers, the Yare and the Bure. There's not much for the children. No amusements there.

But that was not always the case. One day, when a young Victoria had been Britain's queen for only eight years, the Bure was the place to be and it was very much for the children.

Handbills distributed about the town during the morning of Friday, 2 May 1845 announced that Nelson, a clown with Cooke's Equestrian Circus, 'would at five in the afternoon pass from the drawbridge on the Quay to Vauxhall Gardens, on the Bure river, in a washing tub drawn by four real geese, elegantly harnessed'.

Entertainments in Yarmouth, then, were not as many as they are today. There was already excitement, especially amongst the children, that a circus was in town. Nelson's show was to be an added thrill, and a free one.

Despite pouring rain, thousands of people gathered on each side of the river as five o'clock approached. But the best place to see, as the unique performance neared its end, was from a suspension bridge over the Bure.

Until recently, there had been a ferry and then, to move with the times, it had been replaced by the bridge. Just a year before, in expectation of an increase in pedestrians using it to go to and from the new railway station at Vauxhall, a four foot wide footway had been added on each side, outside the bridge's chains. The whole thing was meant to be temporary. A new bridge was to be erected once negotiations were completed between the owners of the bridge and the railway company and the necessary Act of Parliament had been passed.

On that wet May afternoon several hundred people – in reports numbers vary from 300 to 600, but *The Times* said 600 – packed onto the bridge. It was of strong construction and was capable of carrying a much greater weight – but only if it was evenly distributed. It was not.

Everyone was crowded together on the south side, some even climbing onto the bridge's chains and supports, to get a clear view of Nelson as he appeared. Very few stood on the north side where he would be difficult to see. He came into sight, and it was just as promised in the handbills. The harnessed geese were there. Nelson was in his washtub, waving and laughing. A shout went up. 'Here they come!' And then, almost in the same moment, came screams, from those on the bridge and from those on the banks of the river as they saw the disaster before them.

The chains of the bridge on the south side snapped one after another, like the explosions of a Chinese cracker, too quickly for anyone on the bridge to even think of what was happening. In the words of one local newspaper, 'the bridge fell on that side like letting down the leaf of a table'. One moment everyone was marvelling at the spectacle and the next the whole mass of people was plunged into the river.

All together, going with the slope of the bridge platform, they shot straight down. Still together, they piled one on top of another, side by side, forming a bank that 'literally dammed up the waters of the river'. Children had been brought to the front of the crowd to get the best view. They were at the bottom of the pile, the bank of bodies. The water rose to swamp the remains of the bridge where a few people still clung to a chain until they too fell. But one man clung on. He survived and, later, his tale would be told.

It was a quayside. Boats were on hand. Almost at once, twenty-five were on the scene and the saving of lives began, hauling those at the top of the dam of bodies into the boats, taking them to Vauxhall Gardens and returning for more.

On the west side of the river, twenty-seven lucky little girls were saved and taken to the safety of the gardens where they were put to bed until, beginning to recover, their beds were taken by others. On the east side, people rescued were taken into nearby houses for medical treatment.

Boats and rescuers continued their work until half past nine, 'doing their utmost to save the lives of the uppermost of those immersed' before the turn of the tide. When that neared, nets were put on each side of the bridge to stop any bodies being carried out to sea. In all, 'the efforts made to save the victims were noble and self forgetful'.

Heroes emerged, one being that last man left clinging to the bridge. He 'remained suspended above the water' until

> ...a female below clutched at his feet and succeeded in reaching them. The brave fellow looked down and, though in fearful peril himself, encouraged her to hold tight, and she was rescued. The man refused to get into the boat, telling the occupants to pick up those who were floating about the river. Subsequently, however, he was obliged to release his hold and fell into the stream, but a rope was thrown to him immediately and he was brought ashore.

A mother was equally brave. She held her child's clothes in her teeth and paddled them both to safety. Once, in a similar situation in the 1960s *Batman* television series, Batman said to Robin, 'You owe your life to dental hygiene.' I am sure that that mother was glad that she had good teeth. But another mother was less fortunate. She was picked up with a baby in her arms and a toddler held by the hand. 'She had firmly grasped both even in the struggles of death and it was with difficulty they were separated. They were all corpses.'

Some heroes chose to remain anonymous. The son of Charles Sloman, a bookseller well-known in Yarmouth, was saved

> by a gallant fellow whose name could not be ascertained, who was also one of those who fell from the bridge, having extricated himself from the sinking throng he took young Sloman under an arm and another child under the other and succeeded in reaching the shore, saving both.

Word of the accident quickly spread and 'Persons whose children or relatives had gone to see the sight, hearing of the catastrophe, flocked from all parts of the town to make enquiries and to examine the bodies in fearful anxiety. Fathers and mothers were moaning for their children, children for their parents, husbands for their wives, and wives for their husbands.'

And for some their worst imaginings became reality. 'Many a harrowing sight was presented as father, mother or children discovered in the pale and perhaps mutilated face of the lifeless corpse a near and dear relative.'

The bodies of the children were often mutilated, recovered with their heads stuck in the railings where they had been pressing forward to see the clown. Only with great difficulty had they been extricated and some of their heads had been crushed. One child was headless.

Some, the lucky ones, found the person they sought alive, perhaps on the North Quay. But the rescued had been taken to so many places that 'hundreds were left in painful suspense' before they knew that their loved one was safe.

Every doctor in Yarmouth had hurried to the scene to give help, a brewery provided hot water for baths, and blankets were taken from the workhouse to warm the living and to cover the dead. Many of the bodies were taken to the *Norwich Arms*, where they filled every room and the stables. By eleven o'clock that night 'the eyes of seventy-three were closed in death', most of them women and children. The bodies were identified and taken away. On streets all over Yarmouth could be seen bodies on biers, being taken home.

Yarmouth was used to disaster. Ships were wrecked. Lives were lost at sea. But that was a different kind of disaster, felt by everyone. 'The consternation, the agony of the town, is not to be described. It was as if some dread punishment was felt to have fallen upon its habitants. Every face was horror stricken, every eye was dim. Never since the devastating plague of 1739, which swept off two thousand of the inhabitants, has Yarmouth, notwithstanding the numerous shipwrecks, been visited with so dire a calamity.'

At dawn the next morning the search for bodies resumed with both banks of the river crowded by people 'watching in breathless anxiety the efforts of the boatmen and dreading yet hoping in every fresh endeavour to recognise the features of some beloved object. On one side might be seen a group of pale and weeping women with tearful eyes watching the progress of the search, and on the other a party of seamen clasping in their arms the dripping corpse of some favourite child.' When the search ended, seventy-nine bodies had been found and only two remained missing.

An inquest into the disaster opened the next day and the jury would remain at their task until late in the evening 'viewing the bodies of between sixty and seventy of their neighbours and fellow townsmen. They had to traverse the dirtiest and worst-constructed rows in the town, some of which had as many as four or five bodies lying in each. In the great majority of cases they were conducted up staircases of barely sufficient dimensions to enable a full-sized man to pass through and, on arriving at the summit, were shown into the apartment where the body was lain forth, surrounded by relatives uttering the lamentations of distress and misery.' In one small dwelling they found the living, the dying and the dead 'all huddled together' in one room and, in another, 'one unfortunate child, recently shrouded and with a parish coffin beside it, in one corner, another child suffering from the bruises occasioned by the fall in a second, and in the centre of the apartment the mother suckling newborn twins.' At yet another one-room home, where the body of a small boy lay, the jury found a husband and wife and four other children, two of the children 'being over a fire in a very infectious stage of smallpox'. All were 'of the poorer orders', 'honest, hard-working people and not an idler amongst them', who could not afford the cost of a funeral. But immediately the owner of the bridge, C Cory, who had been in London in talks with the railway company about the new bridge when the accident had happened, said that he would pay for all funerals and provide relief where it was needed.

At some point, as the funerals began, unnoticed, the circus quietly left town.

The grave of one nine-year-old victim, George HJ Beloe, can be seen in St Nicholas' churchyard, Great Yarmouth. There is a portrayal of the suspension bridge, now barely discernable, carved into the stone of his memorial. Its verse could be to the memory of every child lost on that day:

Farewell dear boy
no more to press
Thy form of light
and loveliness
and those who gazed on thy
sweet face know it to be
an angels dwelling place
and if that realm
where thou art

now be filled with being
such as thou form
sin free and sorrow free
then heaven must be a
heaven indeed

Chapter 7

Off the Rails

John Ruskin, the late Victorian critic, described the 9,000 miles of railway lines in England as 'the iron veins that traverse our country'. Veins, as we all know, are essential to life.

From the first ever railway accident, causing the death of William Huskisson, President of the Board of Trade, run over by Stephenson's *Rocket* at the opening of the Manchester and Liverpool Railway in September 1830, railways had made the news, and carried all before them. They influenced the entire economy and the lives of everyone. It was the first railway system in the world.

Between 1845 and 1847, the years of the most frantic development, 576 companies were set up and over 8,700 miles of new track agreed, and fortunes were being made speculating in railway shares.

After those veins of Ruskin's came the capillaries feeding into them, with thousands of branch lines laid until even the remotest villages had their own railway station. Rural, agricultural, maritime East Anglia benefitted greatly.

And each station had its own clock. For the first time, thanks to the railways, all clocks in the country were synchronised. A passenger could use a timetable, catch his train at the stated time, be taken to wherever he wanted to go and arrive at the stated time, on some trains at a cost of only a penny a mile.

The railways soon became one of the largest employers of men, and women, in the country and new careers came into being – on the trains, at signal boxes and at the railway stations. The jobs were steady and carried a bit of status. Employees were trusted and trusty. They had goods and mail to safeguard as well as passengers, and they had to keep to that new national time. They were aware of their responsibilities. They were proud of their reliability.

But, as aware as they were, that proved not to be enough in East Anglia on more than one occasion.

On the Great Eastern line between Norwich and Brundall on the evening of 10 September 1874 what was shown was not reliability but laxity and human frailty at their most deadly.

The Great Eastern had a problem. That new commodity, accurate time. Synchronised as clocks were it could not get its timing right. Its trains could be counted on to get where they were going, but late, earning the company the name of Slow But Sure.

Brundall, between Norwich and Yarmouth, was the crossing point for trains going in opposite directions on a single-track line. It worked well, but difficulties could arise when one or other of the trains was late and a decision had to be made on how long a train should be kept waiting for the other. From Brundall, a new stretch of line had been laid to make it double-track, but on 10 September it still had to be inspected. So the established procedure remained in effect. Each evening, the 8.40 up mail train from Yarmouth to Lowestoft would wait at Brundall until the 9.10 down express from London Liverpool Street to Yarmouth went through before being allowed to continue.

Both were long trains of thirteen and fourteen carriages that evening and both were carrying a lot of passengers. The weather was wet and dreary and, as usual, the London express was late. The mail waited, a curbed giant, hissing and steaming in the rain. And then William Platford, the stationmaster, received a message from Norwich Thorpe. The mail could be sent on because the express was late.

There had been a telegraph installed along the line for twenty-six years, the first one in the country, and it had been a boon, adding to safety if not to timekeeping. It was of especial use in single-track working and there had not been an accident in all those twenty-six years. Platford telegraphed his reply and sent the mail on its way.

Regular passengers on the mail were not surprised that they had waited at Brundall and had not seen the express go through. It happened when it was late. No one had any qualms about it, and neither did Platford. But hardly had he waved and whistled away the mail when the truth hit those at Norwich that a mistake had been made and the worst had happened. The mail had left Brundall and the express had been allowed to leave Norwich. Both trains were on the same single-track line, pounding towards each other and disaster.

They met at Thorpe, almost on a bridge over the river Yare, each going at full speed. The collision, 'like a thunderclap', heard all over the area, forced the mail over the top of the express, the front carriages piling up.

Some reports say that they reached twenty feet high before they and the engine rolled over.

Thomas Clarke and Frederick Sewell, driver and fireman of the express, were killed, as was a mule in the first goods van behind the engine. Its eleven carriages and two brake vans were shattered.

John Prior and James Light, driver and fireman of the mail, were also killed. The goods van behind their engine had held tons of cod. Cod were everywhere, flung far and wide, but, to an extent, the fish-packed van had served as a shock absorber. Passengers at the front of the train had been killed. Those just a little way back, saved by cod, had just a few cuts and bruises.

More than twenty passengers died at the scene or later and over seventy were injured. Of four doctors on the Yarmouth to Lowestoft train one was killed, but Dr Eade of Lowestoft survived to help others. His written account of the disaster and its immediate aftermath is graphic:

> Immediately upon the shock I felt that my carriage had come to a sudden standstill, then the compartment in which I was sitting seemed to diminish itself in its dimensions, at the same time as the carriage turned sideways. Then I knew no more until I picked myself up from the wet grass of a meadow, into which I suppose I had been thrown. I collected myself together and was able to appreciate at once that the night was dark, that rain was falling fast, and that steam was roaring from the funnel of an engine, which was standing in dangerous proximity to my person.

Although injured, he then began to check other passengers, some trapped in the wreckage. Realising that many were in a bad way he went into a nearby house to clean his own head wound and his hands before starting to treat them. He had a shot of brandy and then he was back at the scene giving what aid he could.

The sound of the crash had brought Thorpe residents to the scene. They were to make heroic efforts to help the victims. As the local public house, *The Tuns*, took in some of the injured, Dr Eade worked non-stop, using pieces of wood from wrecked carriages to splint the numerous fractures.

The Norwich stationmaster, Sproul, had at once sent cabs to collect doctors in Norwich and had put on a special train to take them to Thorpe to join Eade. They worked through the night in teeming rain, trackside bonfires lighting a scene of horror. The train worked a shuttle service taking the injured into Norwich. Many went to the Norwich and Norfolk Hospital, which could barely cope – with the influx of anxious friends and relatives of those injured more than with the injured themselves. Some of the dead had been so mutilated that they were 'without a whole bone'.

Among those who survived, trapped in the wreckage, was a Norwich dentist, Richard White. He was pinned under a carriage for almost four hours while rescuers worked to extricate him, mainly by sawing through wood. In his own words he was, 'like a man in a coffin bottom upwards' and was in such pain that a doctor soaked a handkerchief in brandy, put it on the end of a stick, and managed to poke it through the wreckage near enough for him to take welcome sucks.

A four-year-old girl was found alive on a cushion of fish, but a six-week-old baby was amongst the dead. John Betts, stoker on the Yarmouth train, died in hospital five days after the accident. But he may have found living hard. The baby had been his, dead in the arms of his dead wife.

As many of those in hospital began to recover the funerals of the dead took place, a sad finale to the worst head-on collision in the history of British railways. While the funeral of Thomas Clarke, engine driver of the express, was taking place in a chapel beside the railway, an express thundered by. It was too much for his widow to bear. She 'became hysterical and needed to be removed from the building'.

For twenty-six years the telegraph, a Cooke and Wheatstone system, had kept the line safe. There was a routine to its operation. At Brundall the station master controlled it and at Norwich a teenaged clerk acted on instructions from the station inspector. Instructions had to be written on a message pad and signed and entered in the record book. At Brundall, the station master would hand a message to the guard who would tell the engine driver that he had permission to proceed. At Norwich, the inspector would hand a signed instruction to the driver. It was a system that had worked well until just after nine o'clock that night when the day inspector, Parker, had just gone off duty and Albert Cooper, the night inspector, had come on.

It was usual to hold the mail for twenty-five minutes and then, if the express had still not arrived, to let it go. The twenty-five minutes would have been up at 9.35. At 9.22 Cooper went to the telegraph office and verbally told the clerk, John Robson, to send the mail from Brundall.

Robson wrote it down, but Cooper left without signing the order, as he should have. At 9.23 the express arrived. Parker had already made out the order allowing it to proceed but when Cooper came up he checked with him that the mail had not been sent. Cooper's reply was: 'No, certainly not. Let's get the train away as soon as possible.' So, the express was sent on its way at 9.30.

Two men at Norwich were responsible for the head-on collision. Robson had telegraphed a message without a signature of authorisation, and Cooper had lied about sending the mail.

At the coroner's inquest into the deaths the jury found both Robson and Cooper guilty of manslaughter, but the coroner singled out Robson for blame.

When the case came before Norwich Assizes in April 1875 it was Robson who was acquitted and Cooper who was found guilty. He was sentenced to eight months imprisonment. In *The Times*, after the court case, the GERs failure to keep time was said to be 'the radical error'.

There were timekeeping problems, too, on the evening of Friday, 21 January 1876, sixteen months after the Thorpe crash. But, on that occasion, there was a reason. The weather. A freezing gale swept a dense blizzard over the whole eastern region, a blinding snowstorm of unprecedented severity.

It was no surprise that a slow, thirty-seven-wagon coal train, bound for London, was eighteen minutes late leaving the New England yards at Peterborough. It left at 5.53. But behind it was the southbound *Flying Scotsman*, running almost on time. It left Peterborough at 6.24.

The coal train was ahead of it and in its way, but there were sidings that it could be shunted into to allow it to pass. The first was at Holme, and signals were set for it to stop and reverse off the main line, but it just went by. It was still all right. There were two signal boxes without telegraph, at Conington and Wood Walton, but a message could be got to Abbots Ripton, six and a half miles ahead. It could be stopped there.

The coal train reached Abbots Ripton. Its driver, Joseph Bray, knew that the *Scotsman* was behind him and he slowed, expecting to be stopped, but the signal was clear. It was white when he had thought that it would be red.

In the Abbots Ripton box the signalman, Charles Johnson, became aware that something had gone wrong. He had set the levers to red but the signal had not changed from white. He went out with a red hand lamp to stop the coal train and started it shunting back into the siding. The *Scotsman* was approaching fast, white signals all the way. But that was all right. Johnson knew that it would be stopped at Wood Walton because he had not sent a message that the line was clear.

When notification that the line ahead was clear was not received at Wood Walton the signal was set to red. It stayed white and the *Scotsman* raced by.

Bray had backed thirty-one of his wagons into the siding when the express roared through the snow whiteout. The collision, with six wagons still on the main line, flung the engine of the express onto its right side with its tender across the down main line. The coaches followed.

Both lines were blocked. Immediately, Johnson tried to contact the Huntingdon signal box, but he couldn't get through. Stukeley, two and a half miles to the south, did not have a telegraph, so he sent an 'obstruction danger' five-bell signal. Both lines were blocked at Abbots Ripton and two more expresses were on their way there – the 5.30 from King's Cross to Leeds and the Manchester to London which had left Peterborough at 6.39, fifteen minutes behind the *Flying Scotsman*.

As the *Flying Scotsman* had roared by, Signalman Rose at Wood Walton had realised that there must be a signalling breakdown. Every signal in the area, with their slot-in-a-post mechanisms, was snow-packed and stuck on white, but there was also ice several inches thick on the wires that changed the signals. It was impossible to change them.

He used his red lamp to warn the Manchester to London and it stopped before Abbots Ripton. The Leeds-bound train was not so lucky. As Johnson's five-bell signal sounded it was passing the Stukeley box. Just a few seconds earlier and that signal could have saved it from disaster.

Great Northern express engines had open cabs. Conditions in the blizzard must have been appalling, but driver Will Wilson was determined to reach Leeds on time. He had been four minutes late at Huntingdon. He was heading for Abbots Ripton at full speed and steam.

There was a complete signalling failure and an approaching express to warn. The undamaged coal train engine at Abbots Ripton was uncoupled. Bray ordered his fireman to go forward on the down line with detonators. He and his guard, Hunt, picked him up as they steamed, full speed ahead, towards Stukeley to raise the alarm. But it was too late. They heard the Leeds express coming. The whistle was sounded, red lamps were waved, the detonators on the line exploded, and Wilson got the message – when he was about 200 yards too near the crash. He had too short a distance in which to stop.

None of the locomotives involved in this disaster had brakes. If an engine needed to stop, the driver sent a whistle signal to the guard in the brake van and he applied the brakes. The Leeds express had two guards and two brake vans. It was being hauled by a Stirling Eight Foot Single express locomotive, the speedster of the day designed to operate the fastest passenger service in the world, and yet they were built without brakes. Both brake vans applied their brakes. The engine was put into reverse. Speed was reduced, but not enough. It hit the wreckage at quarter speed.

The disaster at Abbots Ripton killed thirteen and injured twenty-four. A Board of Trade inquiry highlighted causes that had repercussions far beyond East Anglia and led to a review of the entire railway system and the introduction of improvements. New signals and signalling systems were developed. The practice of leaving signals white until changed to red was scrapped. They were to be left on red. And "all clear" was no longer to be white, the colour of snow. It was to become green. There was to be a telegraph between all signal boxes and, at last, engines were to have brakes.

Today, Christmas is a time for reunions. Over a century ago, in 1892, it was just the same. Where now airports and motorways are jammed with holiday traffic, people journeying to family, friends and festivities, then it was the railways.

On Christmas Eve the 6.27 left Lowestoft and, after several stops, it had over fifty passengers on board. It was to call at Barnby and, finally, Beccles. Coming in the opposite direction was an express which had left London at 12.30, bound for Lowestoft. Both were due to reach the box at Barnby, about five miles from Lowestoft, at the same time, just before 7pm.

The arrangements on the single-track line were for the slow train to run onto a loop at Barnby to allow the express to pass. If it had not reached the loop a signal would halt the express until it had. The engine driver had to be aware of that although, on most occasions, the express rattled through unhalted.

It was a freezing evening and fog was dense over the surrounding marshes. It was so dense that from just a few yards away the signal was invisible. The express driver, Borrett, only realised that he had passed it without seeing if he had right of way when he saw Barnby box. He braked, but the rails were slippery. The fog had made them wet and the wet had frozen to a patina of ice. His train hardly responded.

The slow train was about to run onto the loop when there was the express, wheels screaming over the irons. One moment a foggy blankness and, the next, the inevitable.

They met with a massive collision. The engine of the Beccles-bound train had been travelling tender first. It rebounded from the first impact, went forward again, and then went up and over the express engine until its tender stood almost on end. The first two carriages behind the engine were shattered into matchwood. The engine of the express was blasted into the middle of a third-class carriage, and another carriage was telescoped, trapping passengers in a mangle of debris.

Amos Beamish and his wife lived nearby. They heard the crash and the cries of passengers. He grabbed a huge hammer and ran across a fog-bound marsh. Strong and muscular, he set to work and freed some trapped passengers. Others he could not free. He ran back home to fetch his saw and then continued his rescue work.

Eight or nine men were in the bar of the *Barnby Swan* enjoying a drink and a warm before a fire when a boy came in, his face covered in blood, and raised the alarm. Mr Holt, the landlord, harnessed his pony and trap, found a lantern and a bottle of brandy, and all raced to the scene while Mrs Holt made ready to receive the injured. Another trap was sent to Dr Hunter at Carlton. Hunter would be the first of at least eight local doctors to attend the accident.

Of the work of Beamish, and Holt and his customers, the *East Suffolk Gazette* said, 'prodigies of human deeds were performed by these simple country folk'.

As news of the accident was flashed on the wire, the station master at Barnby arranged for a special train to be sent to the scene. On board were members of the recently-formed Great Eastern Railway Ambulance Class. Barnby station was closed by the police and the platform was cleared in readiness for the return of the train with the injured.

Word had quickly spread and a crowd had gathered, pressed behind hastily-erected barriers as they waited for news of loved ones. It was 9.15 before engine number 28 slowly and steadily drew in with its 'load of bandaged and bloodstained humanity'. Cabs and all available conveyances were waiting to take them to hospital.

Some of them were taken to the *Swan*, where Mrs Holt had prepared a room, so well that she was amongst those to receive a special mention from the coroner at the inquest into the deaths of three men, one of them a passenger:

> Too much cannot be said in praise of the behaviour of the Barnby folks on this occasion, they worked with a will with great self-denial, the bitterness of the night, and so many of them doffed their garments that the wounded might be made warmer and more comfortable.
>
> Amos Beamish was of immense value and the way in which he moved huge masses of timber and held them whilst the dead and injured were carefully removed was quite magnificent to behold. He was the one to find the body of Lake, the guard of the Beccles train, and in other ways he proved of immense assistance on the scene of the disaster.
>
> Mr and Mrs Holt also behaved hard and well and she by her womanly instinct and thought proved of as much service as any management. Her house presented all the appearance of a hospital.

All had worked through into Christmas Day. There can have been none other like it in Suffolk history.

There had been two serious fires and over a hundred lesser ones on express passenger trains between 1949 and 1951 when there was one more at Huntingdon on 14 July 1951.

The train was the 3.45 from King's Cross to Leeds, the *West Riding*, and what took place was somewhere between an horrific disaster and a Laurel and Hardy comedy.

The train was made up of articulated, centre-corridor coaches, each seating sixty-four passengers. About forty-five minutes into its journey a female passenger in the rearmost left-hand seat of the first coach noticed a coil of smoke rising between her armrest and the side of the coach.

She told a passing fifteen-year-old pantry boy, selling ice cream. He told the restaurant car manager. The manager opened the window of a door and looked out. He could not see any smoke, but he told the guard. The guard came and had a look. Smoke was, by then, snaking out from beneath the carpet. He decided that it was coming from a hot axle box.

The train was nearing Huntingdon, where it was not due to stop. The guard decided that the best thing to do would be for a message to be thrown from a window as they went through Huntingdon asking for the train to be stopped at Peterborough, half an hour away. It must be wrapped around a weight to prevent it being blown away. A stone. But he did not have a stone. Well, a potato, then.

At a Ministry of Transport inquiry a few days later the restaurant car manager told what happened:

> The next thing I remember was the guard asking me for a potato so that he could throw a message inside it from the train. He had been to see the smoke and was suggesting that we should have the train stopped for examination at Peterborough. I did not have a potato, but the guard threw a message out at the signal box.

While he was doing that a passenger came from the front of the train and said that things were worsening, there was thick black smoke and a flame, and something needed to be done about it. He wanted to pull the communication cord, but he couldn't find one. One was found in a vestibule and pulled, twenty minutes after the smoke had first been noticed.

The train stopped within two minutes and, as it did, the fire, later found to have been caused by a live coal trapped under a floor, spread up the sides of the coach and onto the roof and over sixty passengers scrambled to get out, blocking the corridor. There was crush inside the coach and fire outside. The only thing to do was to smash the windows and jump.

When the train stopped the driver saw broken glass 'and men and women diving out onto the ballast'. As they left the burning coach it was, he said, 'soldiers and sailors first and women last'.

Detail was added by the locomotive's fireman:

> Immediately we stopped, smoke started coming out of the compartment ventilators at the rear of the second coach and people and suitcases and babies and everything started coming out. Lord knows what came out.

Twenty people were injured, but none seriously. The fire spread to destroy four coaches.

The resourceful guard, too ill to attend the inquiry, inadvertently brought in safer trains. There was to be a new design of coach with an emergency exit, fire extinguishers and more visible communication cords. Less inflammable materials were to be used, and there was to be fire drill for all staff.

Not acted upon was a suggestion that guards should be given weighted envelopes in which to throw out messages at stations. There was no mention of protective headgear for the recipient.

When Queen Victoria, towards the end of her reign, took her first ride in a train, a short journey from Slough to Windsor, *The Times* commended her bravery. But its advice to Her Majesty was 'we must insist with respect that these Royal excursions should for preference be wholly abandoned or but occasionally resorted to'.

Pity. The train would have been so useful in getting her to the Scotland she loved quickly and safely. But perhaps *The Times* was right. There had been that accident to the *Flying Scotsman* in 1876, hadn't there?

And on Sunday, 5 March 1967, on exactly the same stretch of line between Huntingdon and Peterborough, the same train made the headlines again. It was derailed.

The overnight express had left King's Cross at 10.30, hauled by a Deltic diesel locomotive that drew its eleven coaches effortlessly on their way to Edinburgh at about 85mph. An hour later it was on the Down Fast line of the East Coast Main Line, ten miles north of Huntingdon, near the village of Conington, with 147 passengers on board, when the last six coaches were flung onto their sides. The front five coaches, including the sleeping car, were unaffected and travelled a further half mile down the line. The train had just passed a signal box – Conington South.

Dawn, after several hours of hard, skilled and traumatic work by emergency services, showed a desolate scene, with debris and personal belongings spread along 500 yards of line. Five passengers were dead, killed instantly, and eighteen were seriously injured. All had been in three of the last four coaches. Some had been thrown through windows or had been trapped inside the wreckage. Others had managed to crawl out to wander about, dazed and shocked, until found by police.

The one question everyone needed answering was – what happened? One man, perhaps, had the answer. An eyewitness. The express had just passed Conington South box. The signalman there was twenty-one-year-old Alan John Frost of Dogsthorpe, Peterborough. *The Flying Scotsman* had been travelling at about 80mph past his box, he said, when, 'There was a rumbling and suddenly I saw the last coach keel over.'

Jack Wright of Grantham, the train's guard, said, 'I heard bumping and a violent jerk. The lights went out and my carriage went straight onto its side. I was slung from my seat. I pulled myself together and climbed out of the window.'

Uninjured, he had run 200 yards back down the line to the Conington South box where he found Frost calm and seemingly unaware of the need for urgent action until he shouted at him, 'Stop all roads. The train is on its side and I've dead and dying passengers.'

Frost, who had seen and heard the derailment taking place in front of him, should not have needed to be told. But Frost's behaviour in other respects was far from what it should have been. When the express had not passed the next box, Conington North, its signalman had phoned Frost to ask if anything had happened to it. Frost's cool reply had been, 'The signals are in order and the train appears to have stopped', when, just beyond his box, a frightful accident had taken place.

Even as the line was being cleared to allow single-track use for the southbound *Flying Scotsman* to go through it was becoming clear that Frost needed questioning further.

Frost, although young to be in sole charge of an important signal box, knew the rules and regulations and his responsibilities. Edwin Howell, his superior, said, 'I thought he had a very good knowledge for a young lad', but he had just reprimanded him. He had called him to King's Cross for a sharp word for allowing a slow train to run on a fast track. It had been classed as 'an error of judgement', affecting the punctuality of trains but not their safety.

Had another error of judgement derailed the *Flying Scotsman?*

It was up to John Robson, a signals and communications supervisor based at Peterborough, to find out. He knew Frost well and found him 'acting normally' after the accident. Nothing had been touched when he went into the box. All levers were where they should be but, on one, there was a slick of oil showing that it had been moved recently. Robson was sure that it should not have been. He checked the timetable. He was right. It should not have been moved in the past two days. It operated a set of points 85ft north of Conington South box to close the Down Fast line, the one that the *Flying Scotsman* had been on, and open the Down Goods line.

Numerous safeguards were built into the points and signalling system to ensure that accidents were not caused by human error. When the signal was at green on the Down Fast a safeguard made it impossible to operate the Down Goods points, and both the driver and the second man on the Deltic were certain that it had been green as they passed it.

But, Robson began to consider, could Frost have beaten the safeguard? It would have meant moving three levers in less than two seconds. Could it have been done? When tests showed that it could be done by an experienced signalman the police were involved.

Investigations concluded that Frost, accidentally or deliberately, had operated those three levers, opening the points while the *Flying Scotsman* had been going over them and derailing it. Frost denied doing so but, when it became impossible to go on with a denial, he said that he had done it accidentally while 'swinging' on the levers. If that was or was not so would have to be determined in court.

Frost, by then twenty-two years old and a Royal Engineers bandsman, was tried at Nottingham Assizes at the end of November 1968 on charges of manslaughter, endangering the safety of passengers by unlawfully operating a signal and points mechanism, and wilful neglect of his duties. What he had done, the prosecution claimed, amounted to 'the grossest form of negligence'.

There was technical detail for the members of the jury to come to terms with and, to help them, and perhaps for the only time in a British court, a 10ft stretch of model railway was set up to demonstrate what had happened. To help further, a signal lever was also set up in the court room and the ten men on the jury spent some time operating it to see how the signal and points system and the safety mechanism worked. Yes. Ten men. In the sexist sixties, trains were boys' toys, even in a court. The men operated the signal. The two women on the jury just watched.

The trial lasted for eleven days. Frost had pleaded not guilty but when the judge instructed the jury to acquit him on the manslaughter charge, because he may have accidentally caused the derailment, he changed his pleas to guilty on all other charges. He was sentenced to two years imprisonment.

At one point he considered selling his story to a newspaper and making a lot of money. The title was to be *How I Wrecked the Scotsman*.

Most of us, from time to time, make a journey by train through East Anglia or elsewhere in the country. The train may be overcrowded, or it may be late, but the chances are that it will be safe. Wont it? Conington may be haunted by the dead, as some claim it to be, and Thorpe, Barnby and Abbots Ripton too, but if any ghosts are about surely they belong to yesterday.

Other Norman towers fell at Bury St Edmunds but this one, built by Abbot Anselm between 1120 and 1140 survives today. Author's collection

The octagon and lantern at Ely Cathedral, an inspirational replacement for a central Norman tower which collapsed in 1322. The author

The gates into Norwich have gone, although parts of the walls remain. This was the site of St Stephen's Gate, the approach to the city from London – and Wymondham. No herald needed today to demand its opening. The author

A plaque marks where Robert Kett was 'hanged in chains' over the walls of Norwich castle. Four hundred years later the citizens of Norwich forgave him. The author

The site of King Charles' Palace, 'plac'd in a dirty streete', Newmarket High Street. The author

Burwell village sign. The author

Sign for Cuckolds Row, Burwell, site of the barn where the fire occurred on 8 September 1727. The author

A plaque in Cuckolds Row commemorates the fire of 1727 and the tragic loss of so many villagers' lives. The author

NEAR THIS SPOT STOOD THE BARN WHERE 78 PEOPLE (51 CHILDREN AND 27 ADULTS) DIED IN A FIRE DURING A PUPPET SHOW ON 8TH SEPTEMBER 1727

BURWELL HISTORY SOCIETY 2005 BURWELL PARISH COUNCIL

The 'flaming heart' memorial to the victims of the Burwell fire, in St Mary's churchyard. The author

Here, a suspension bridge over the river Bure, North Quay, Great Yarmouth, collapsed on 2 May 1845 with the loss of 79 lives, most of them children. The public house on Riverside is called *The Suspension Bridge*. The author

St Nicholas churchyard, Great Yarmouth, where some of the victims of the 1845 bridge collapse are buried. Author's collection

The suspension bridge is carved into the headstone on the grave of nine-year-ol victim George HJ Belde, in St Nicholas churchyard, Great Yarmouth. The autho

Until 1923, Flying Scotsman was the name of the London-Edinburgh train that had started running in 1862. In 1923 the name was given to the apple-green LNER Atlantic engine hauling it. Soon to become iconic, it is here seen racing through Huntingdon in the 1930s. By the time of the derailment the *Flying Scotsman* locomotive was a Deltic diesel.
Huntingdonshire Archives/Local Studies PH/48/174

Injured passengers being removed from the wreckage of the railway crash in severe winter conditions at Abbots Ripton, on 21 January 1876.
Cambridgeshire Collection

A trackside memorial where thirteen passengers lost their lives in the railway crash at Abbots Ripton, Huntingdon, on 21 January 1876.
Huntingdonshire Archives/ Local Studies DC59

Huntingdon railway station where on 14 July 1951, an enterprising guard with a train on fire threw out a message. He would have preferred to throw out a potato.
The author

Gathering in the sheaves by boat, Ramsey, August 1912. Cambridgeshire Collection

More than the harvest was in danger in August 1912 as the river Ouse burst its bank to inundate the land. Would a few sandbags bridge the gap? Cambridgeshire Collection

Sandbags again, and plenty of them, to build up the banks of the
old Bedford at Welney, March 1947. Cambridgeshire Collection

The Cambridge-Ely railway line flooded at Little Thetford, March 1947.
Cambridgeshire Collection

St Margaret's church, King's Lynn, flooded on many occasions. Bad as the 1953 tidal surge was, it was flooded to a greater depth in 1978.
Author's collection

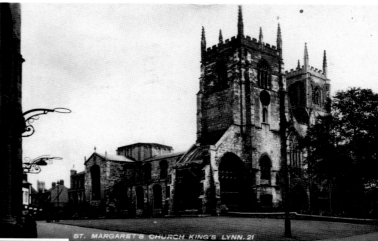

ST. MARGARET'S CHURCH KING'S LYNN. 21

HIGH WATER

HIGH WATER
31st JANUARY 1953

HIGH WATER

HIGH WATER
20th MARCH 1961

HIGH WATER
1st MARCH 1949

Five flood level markers outside the west door of St Margaret's, King's Lynn. 1953 was not the highest. Will there be another? The author

Coastal defences all along the east coast are formidable and a constant watch is kept. Here at Felixstowe, a Napoleonic martello tower is used for that purpose. Before it is part of the flood wall along the shore. The heavy metal gate would be closed in times of danger. The author

On 19 January 1915, German Zeppelin L3 bombed St Peter's Plain, Great Yarmouth, wrecking the villa on the left. Two people in the street became the first ever British fatalities caused by attack from the air. The author

An airship over Emmanuel Street, Cambridge, in 1915. Cambridgeshire Collection

Men from the Cambridge area drafted in to help in the aftermath of a serious Zeppelin raid on Lowestoft in April 1915. Cambridgeshire Collection

Lowestoft endured many bombardments causing extensive damage. Author's collection

St Mary's Square, Newmarket, and the *Five Bells* where the third bomb fell during the Zeppelin raid on 24 April 1916. The second bomb fell to the left of the trees, at the bottom of Icewell Hill. The author

Sparrow's Nest Park, Lowestoft, now. A small museum and commemoration of the work of the Royal Naval Patrol Service is on the left with a mine beside the flag staff. The author

Plaque on the wall of the Royal Naval Patrol Service museum at Sparrow's Nest Park, Lowestoft. The author

A memorial bench marks the spot in Clacton where the crash of a minelaying Heinkel caused the first civilian fatalities of the Second World War on the British mainland. The author

NEAR THIS SPOT ON TUESDAY 30TH APRIL 1940 A HEINKEL BOMBER CRASHED KILLING THE GERMAN CREW AND MR & MRS GILL OF VICTORIA ROAD, WHO WERE THE FIRST CIVILIAN CASUALTIES OF WORLD WAR II ON THE BRITISH MAINLAND

Ten bombs were dropped in Newmarket High Street in an attack by a Dornier bomber on 18 February 1941. Bombs nine and ten fell in front of The King Edward VII Memorial Hall on the right and the former Doric cinema on the left. The author

Most of Norwich's historic buildings survived the Baedeker raids of 1942. The Norman cathedral survived unscathed, a miracle as it was a big target. Author's collection

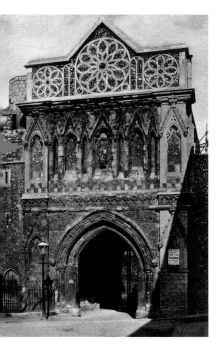

Another survivor, along with Norwich's cathedral, was the fourteenth-century entrance into the Cathedral Close, The Ethelbert Gate. The original thirteenth-century gate was destroyed by rioting townspeople. Hitler's raids in the Second World War barely shook it. Author's collection

Norwich Grammar School, one of the oldest in the world, established at the time of King Henry VIII, was surrounded by the numerous incendiaries to fall in the Cathedral Close during the Baedeker raids of 1942. Today, enlarged, it is the Norwich School. Author's collection

Soham Station before the explosion on 2 June 1944. The tall figure on the right is signalman Frank Bridges, killed when the bombs detonated. Cambridgeshire Collection

Soham Station after the explosion on 2 June 1944. American servicemen are at work filling the large crater. Within eighteen hours new track would be laid and the line reopened to traffic. Cambridgeshire Collection

Gimbert Road, named in recognition of the bravery of engine driver Ben Gimbert in saving the town of Soham, 2 June 1944. The author

The saving of Soham was not forgotten fifty years after the event. When a town sign was erected in 1994 it featured the exploding train. The author

A Canberra PR9, such as the one which crashed onto the Oxmoor estate, Huntingdon, on 3 May 1977. This one is now outside the main gateway of RAF Wyton. The author

On 3 May 1977, a Canberra PR9 from RAF Wyton crashed onto Norfolk Road on the Oxmoor estate, Huntingdon. Fire destroyed a terrace of houses and damaged others. Three children died. The author

The *Red Grind* ferry at the *Plough Inn*, Ditton, being recovered from the Cam the day after its capsize on 10 June 1905. Cambridgeshire Collection

The Townsend Thoresen ferry *European Gateway* rolled over onto her starboard side after her collision with the *Speedlink Vanguard* on 19 December 1982. RNLI, Harwich

The *European Gateway* lies in shallow water after her collision with the *Speedlink Vanguard* off Harwich on 19 December 1982. Despite a North Sea gale and personal danger East Anglian men of the sea saved many lives in gallant rescues. Six men aboard the *Gateway* died. RNLI, Harwich

Chapter 8

And the Waters Prevailed

One thing that East Anglia is about is water, both fresh and salt, and only a fine balance keeps that water under control, a friend and not an enemy. Excessive rain, in the region or beyond it, falling or thawing snow, a high tide, a storm surge – all can cause widespread inundation. When floods caused by heavy rainfall and an exceptional tide occur at the same time, especially if accompanied by a severe gale, a disaster is likely.

As long as there has been recorded history there have been accounts of flooding in East Anglia, inland and on the coast. It was mentioned in *Domesday Book*, and in the *Anglo-Saxon Chronicles* of 1099 is written, 'the sea flood sprang up to such a height, and did so much harm, as no man remembered it ever did happen before'. But it had happened before, and it would go on happening again and again all along the coast from the Wash down into Essex, through to the present day.

At any time, rivers may flood in town and countryside, the fenland waterways system may become overwhelmed or, most disastrously of all, a storm surge of gale-driven, mountainous seas may funnel down the North Sea and onto the region's exposed east coast. Here are just some of the more recent, twentieth century, instances when all of those things have happened.

There has always been a fight, from Roman times onwards, to keep parts of the region dry. It has needed unyielding control and vigilance but still, from time to time, the elements, always with the potential to be greater than man, have shown that water is a relentless foe.

It claimed East Anglia as its own in August 1912, when rain fell in Biblical amounts. A warning to build an ark would have been welcome, but East Anglians were not to be as forewarned as Noah. It was the wettest month of the new century, of the reign of the new king, George V. It just rained and rained. Previous months had been unsettled and cold, not like summer at all, but August brought an almost continual downpour and, towards its end, farmers everywhere were facing the total loss of their harvest.

There had been a few brief breaks in the rain but, on the afternoon of Saturday 24 August, it became torrential and was driven into impenetrable curtains by a fierce gale. The outlook was not good either. The long-range forecast was 'distinctly unfavourable'. There was 'every indication of a continuance of the watery visitation during the next few days'.

And what a visitation it was, recognised from the start as a disaster in the making, so bad that the *London Daily News and Leader* sent a special correspondent to Huntingdon to report:

> Clouds of a hundred shades of grey, like great wet sponges, hung low all day over the Fen Country. In the morning it rained, the fifth morning in six, but still, like Roman cohorts, conquering, silent, the grey clouds rolled up from the sea. I had come down to see the disaster they were working, and that not here nor there, in this village or in that farm, but wherever the Ouse drained the fat valley lands, wherever its little tributaries ran, and even on the hilltops, where the wind drove the rain merciless into the very heart of the stooks.

Ducks were swimming down the potato drills 'like a string of barges', a man trying to go by boat into Alconbury over flooded fields was 'wrecked on a haycock', a Wisbech farmer had to row across his farmyard to milk his cows and an Essex farmer, facing ruin, committed suicide.

The rain continued. Almost an inch had already fallen in the Haverhill area when, on the morning of Monday, the 26th, 'a great exodus from the town took place, the members of the local juvenile Order of Ancient Shepherds left by their annual excursion for Clacton-on-Sea.' They were drenched to the skin before they started but they were undeterred. They bred them tough in Haverhill. Two troops of the town's Boy Scouts had already left for camp in Felixstowe.

On that Monday record amounts of rain fell – 2ins in Cambridge, nearly 4 in the Waveney Valley, 6 by mid-afternoon around Huntingdon and over 7 at Great Yarmouth – but young members of the Ancient Order of Foresters were as adventurous as the Ancient Shepherds. Several hundred left Cambridge for Great Yarmouth and that 7ins of rain. With many rail services suspended they were lucky to reach their destination, and even luckier to get home again. They had to go via London.

They were more fortunate than passengers from King's Cross to Cromer and Yarmouth on the Great Northern evening express. It went no further than King's Lynn where families bound for their summer holiday by the sea were dumped with their luggage on flooded platforms. If they had travelled from Liverpool Street they would have known what to expect. Notices in booking office windows there read: 'Owing to continuous rains in certain parts of Norfolk the train service is interrupted and trains will be liable for diversion and delay. By Order.'

They were also liable not to get there at all. The engine of a Great Eastern train, trying to reach King's Lynn from Thetford, failed because a wave put out its fire, and a Great Eastern goods train fell through a collapsed viaduct between Fakenham and Walsingham.

The already swollen Ouse rose at the rate of 1ft every 3 hours to over 16ft above normal all along its length. Its bank gave way at Hilgay, Norfolk. Ely riverside was inundated and the *Cutter Inn* and houses in Annesdale put under water and, by the evening of that Monday, streets in St Ives were flooded. On Tuesday morning the water at the fifteenth century Old Bridge in St Ives was an inch above the record high set in a previous disastrous flood in July 1875, and it was still rising.

Every road in the town was affected, but the locals, familiar with the threat of some degree of flood, were staunch. The inhabitants of thirty-eight houses in Victoria Terrace, beyond the bridge in the direction of Hemingford Grey, were up at dawn 'hastily digging potatoes from their gardens and removing fowls, pigs etc., for fear of the rising water.' They had just saved what they could, and themselves, when the flood was rushing through the lower rooms of their houses and they had to retreat upstairs, no doubt with their potatoes, fowls, pigs etc.

August apparently was the excursion season, and the people of St Ives did not want to miss out even with flood on their doorsteps. That morning great numbers of them turned up at the railway station for a planned day trip to Yarmouth and were not happy when told that it had been cancelled, even though it was for their own safety. Bridges along the route were in a dangerous condition.

And if they had gone what would they have found? Yarmouth was much worse off than St Ives. The old Yarmouth seafarers had feared the worst. They had not liked 'the greasy look of the moon'. The barometer had been falling and, by dawn, so had the rain.

As the rain had worsened so had a gale. Trees and telegraph poles were brought down, the streets flooded and tramcars were put out of action, but the 'staying visitors' and day-trippers still battled their way along the prom, determined to enjoy being by the sea.

During the morning a large steamer, the *Egyptian*, was driven onto a sandbank off Yarmouth and the Gorleston Lifeboat braved the seas to rescue the captain's wife and child and ten of the crew. The captain and the rest of the crew stayed aboard, hoping she would refloat on the next flood tide, but conditions became too dangerous in the afternoon and they had to be brought ashore and taken to the Sailors' Home at Gorleston.

Downpour and a violent gale hit Lowestoft. Pedestrians could hardly keep their feet. It was especially bad at the Suffolk Hotel corner where a lady was blown over and 'a perambulator was caught by a sudden gust and capsized, the child fortunately being unhurt as two men and a policeman went to the rescue smartly'. Umbrellas and trees were upended and telegraph poles were 'snapped off like carrots'. Roofs of the Hippodrome and the South Beach Concert Pavilion were ripped off.

The intrepid young Ancient Shepherds from Cambridge perhaps considered it was worth their soaking when they got to Clacton. It was certainly a once-in-a lifetime experience to see the town's drains overcharging and storm water shooting up in fountains before flooding into houses and, if their interest reached as far as learning the cause of such phenomenal rainfall, meteorologists had an answer.

A complex depression had arrived from the Bay of Biscay. It had two barometric minima, one over the Kent coast and one off the west coast of Ireland, while pressure was high over Iceland and the south-west of England. That had amounted to rain, and lots of it, with no immediate chance of a change.

Hearts must have sunk in Norwich on learning that. Norfolk and the Broads were bearing the brunt but, in Norwich, people were 'meeting experiences which have not been equalled within living memory'. What was taking place in the city was total disaster.

The city made national headlines in the Tuesday, 27 August newspapers after the almost unbelievable amount of 6ins of rain had fallen in 11 hours, well over 2ins falling in just 4 hours. The rainfall over 30 hours, into Wednesday, would be over 7ins. Floods rose. Railways and roads were closed and telephones and the telegraph stopped working. Norwich was cut off, on its own.

As in the still-remembered snow-melt floods of November 1878, it was the rising of the river Wensum to overflow and break its banks that was the main cause of the flooding of August 1912 as it ran its swollen course through the oldest parts of the city. It ran for 2 miles from the western limits of Norwich to the Carrow works of Colmans, the famous Norwich mustard manufacturers, on the eastern side.

In a matter of a few hours over 15,000 people were made homeless, with 1,500 given shelter at the Salvation Army Barracks, where officers were still coming to terms with the 'raising to Glory' of their founder and leader, General Booth, who had died just a few days before. The YMCA and several schools also took the homeless in.

The damage to non-domestic premises was city-wide. Of 3,600 buildings flooded, sixty of them were factories. Others were malthouses, warehouses, mills, public houses and shops, including Curl's department store in the market place. Bullard's brewery collapsed and the front of two storeys of the *Norwich Mercury* offices fell, print machinery disappearing into the water – just when there was a headline story to tell. The water and electricity company premises were inundated, but gas remained on tap.

J and J Colman headed the list of donors to a Relief Fund at once set up by the Lord Mayor, giving £1,000 even though the Colman factory had been flooded at great financial loss. Several feet of water had found its way into a cellar and destroyed 650tons of starch. Men worked frantically to save what they could, naked in a wet, mustardy, lamp-lit gloom. In other premises, workers wore bathing suits, as did some of the rescuers in the streets.

Almost everyone today is familiar with Norwich City FC, nicknamed the Canaries. The team wears yellow and there is a canary on the club badge. Norwich, at the time of the 1912 flood, was an important centre for the breeding of canaries – of the feathered kind. As the floods struck many breeders lost valuable stocks of birds, the work of a lifetime, and one species of Norwich canary was wiped out entirely.

Trowse, Heigham, Caslany and the area around Magdalen Street were badly awash. Up to 10ft of water rushed into streets and alleys, dwellings and innumerable small tenements. Across the city there was subsidence, massive holes opening up over old chalk and sandpits. Forty-two bridges came down and thirty-five churches were flooded from crypt to aisle.

Boats, some rowed by YMCA members, were used to ferry supplies to marooned residents or to carry out rescues. Where the water was shallower, horses and carts were used, and bare-legged small boys, trousers turned up but still wearing their jackets and flat caps, paddled, making the most of a novel situation as, on Wednesday, the rain eased at last and the flood level began to dip. As it did so, the bodies of hundreds of drowned rats were revealed, giving the paddlers, no doubt, a few moments for thought.

On Thursday, electricity was restored, trams began to run, and a few trains were getting to Norwich via Wymondham, although they were still unable to go on to the coast. The river went down a further 5ft. Shops re-opened and, of course, the public houses, with mud on their floors and water in their cellars, but not in their beer. Some pubs had stayed open throughout the flood and had had customers to serve.

On Friday, the clean-up of the city began in earnest, a massive task with hardly a house in the city undamaged by wind, rain or flood.

The Relief Fund raised £24,000 in just its first few days, including £150 from the King and Queen and £50 from the Prince of Wales, but much more was needed. It was estimated that losses in Norwich amounted to well over £250,000.

A volume of water such as had never been seen before left behind it filth, damp, devastation and heartbreak. Norwich was a wreck, as were many other places right across East Anglia, but, despite everything, it had come through its days of disaster. And, in one respect, lightly. The flood had taken only three lives – those of a four-month-old baby, snatched from his mother's arms, an asthmatic man who had selflessly made rescue after rescue until, exhausted, he had been taken away by the flow, and an old lady, said to have died of 'fright and shock'. But, perhaps proof that the life of Norwich would go on, several babies had been born in the floods.

The whole of East Anglia would gather itself together, dry itself out, and go on.

Daniel Defoe, in the 1720s, called the Fens 'the sink of no less than thirteen counties.' And he was right. The rivers flowing into and across them carry the surplus water of over 6,000 square miles of surrounding higher land to the sea. After Defoe's time and the draining of the fenlands themselves, the amount of water in transit increased further and could be phenomenal at a time when the Fens themselves were changing.

With the seventeenth century laying dry of the fenlands by Dutchman Cornelius Vermuyden for the Earl of Bedford and his Company of

Adventurers the level of the land in the Fens began to lower, to shrink. In some places the shrinkage was as much as 12ft leaving the river beds well above the land and necessitating the creation of a complex system of banks, dykes and channels to ensure the safe movement of water. Increasingly stronger embankment and means of pumping water had been needed to ensure that the fenland waterways system as a whole could cope. In March 1947, in exceptional weather conditions, it failed to cope.

The winter of 1946-1947, in post-war austerity Britain, had been one of the coldest, wettest and hardest that anyone could remember. There had been weeks of severe frost and snow. The ground in the Fens was frozen to a depth of 18ins. Snow drifts were over 6ft high and, because of the continuing freeze, had not diminished.

And then on 10 March, had come a sudden thaw and on the following day there had been a downpour. Together they had amounted to almost 5ins of wet which the ground was still too frozen to absorb. It ran into the channels at a colossal rate.

The thaw and rain were everywhere in England. All rivers, from the Humber to the Thames, rose and began to run at record highs. Those heading towards the flat Fens were flooding, and, once in the Fens, the absence of gradient would mean that the greatly increased amounts of water they carried would not drain away quickly. The gradient of the Great Ouse was only about 1in in a mile and the flow of water down river was further slowed by the sluice across the Ouse at Denver, designed to control the inflow of high tides.

The rain and melt waters from elsewhere were teeming into the waterways, heading for the Fens, and already there was a battle in prospect. With the thaw and the torrential rain running off into the rivers at an unprecedented rate, pressure quickly built up on the Welland, the Nene and the Ouse, made worse by the fact that some pumps and sluices were still partially frozen. The retaining banks as they passed through the Fens would be severely tested, and some were already weakened, cracked, by the weeks of frost.

Flood patrols were begun along the banks, increased by 14 March as the volumes of water being carried continued to build up. Sandbags were put in place at points where the banks were most in danger of being topped. And then the work of strengthening the banks gained a new urgency on Saturday, 15 March as word reached the Fens of serious floods up river, in the Ouse Valley. Water levels had risen to 6ft above normal. At Bedford 500 homes, shops and offices were under water.

The situation worsened during that Saturday. There was more flooding and, from the flood patrols, came reports of overtopping and, most seriously, of numerous threats of breaches in the banks that were vitally protecting the area's agricultural land. Already riverside houses and the *Cutter* at Ely were flooded, as they had been in 1912. Roads and the railway were flooded at Littleport, The Washes, areas left as safety valves at times of flooding, able to contain excess water, were already overflowing, and roads at Welney and Earith were awash. They were the precursors of what was to become one of the worst human disasters ever to take place in the Fens.

The need to prevent breaches in the banks became of the utmost urgency. All would be saved or lost by that. But the height of the water made it impossible for the tugs and barges bringing reinforcements of clay, gault, to pass beneath the bridges. Eighteen barges sank in the attempt.

Bad as the situation had been on the Saturday it became worse on the Sunday. To the teeming rain and biting cold was added a hurricane force wind, making work atop the slippery banks almost impossible. A wind of 70mph, gusting to 98, was driving waves over men and mud, was blowing out lamps and lifting workers off their feet. Sandbags were being whipped away even as they were placed.

It became certain that the Ouse would flood. People living in areas which would be inundated if its banks blew began to save what belongings they could, ready for evacuation, while outside their homes, many in isolated locations, phone lines and electricity poles were down in a wild, dark world. Debris blocked roads, hampering rescue.

At about 10pm the bank of the river Lark downstream of Prickwillow began to bulge and seemed about to burst. In Burnt Fen, 100 people were evacuated and taken to RAF Mildenhall, while a further ninety went to the Prickwillow WI. Temporarily, the breach was held, but for how long? Just a mile or so away, on the Ouse at Ely, water was being lashed over roads. The road beneath the railway bridge had 3ft of water, as did the station subway.

A gale still blew on Monday, 17 March, driving spray and water over the bank tops, destroying repair work even as it was completed. By then 1,000 men were at work, river and fen men, volunteers and German POWs, but things were worsening in more and more places. Breaches became unavoidable – and then they began.

There was a bad one at Over. It flooded the village, nearby

Willingham, and thousands of acres of good land. There was another one at Little Thetford, near Ely. That one swept two barges through the gap as it went and flooded over 2,000 acres in Thetford and Stretham Fens.

Men who had been battling so long and so hard to save the banks were exhausted. They had reached a point where they knew that they would not be able to go on when - in came the Army. The troops renewed the spirits of everyone and brought a military efficiency to the whole effort. They were up to tackling the worst of incidents.

One of those, unless prevention continued, was that bulging bank at Prickwillow, It remained at bursting point. Barges of gault could not pass beneath Prickwillow Bridge. Supplies had to be taken there by lorry, tipped over its side into barges, and then taken to the site.

While a gigantic effort was under way to save the 11,000 acres of Middle Fen there were disasters elsewhere. The torrent rushing across Over Fen was pouring into the Old West River which itself began to overflow into Hillrow Fen. A domino effect from fen to fen. Soon after midday Hillrow was lost. That had been expected all morning and the evacuation of homeowners and farmers was well advanced. By twilight most of the land had gone. Perhaps half a roof could be seen, or a sodden haystack. Among the last to leave the fen were six Land Army girls bagging potatoes. They stayed on the job until the flood was at their feet. By next morning 3,000 acres were under water.

Still it spread, from Hillrow into Haddenham North Fen. It joined other flood waters near Sutton to cover 3 square miles in depths up to 12ft, then it crept around to Aldreth to join up with the Stretham flood.

Other areas were badly hit, especially Feltwell Fen, and Southery on the banks of the Wissey, and Wissington where a race was on to save 6,000 tons of sugar in the local sugar beet factory.

As the desperate work continued, a press conference was held by WE Doran, Chief Engineer of the Great Ouse Catchment Board. He told of the many breaches, but focussed on what lay ahead:

> We are dependent on the tide situation at Denver for getting the water away. We are now getting on to the spring tides and we are getting more water each night. If more rain comes and further discharges from the Lark, the Little Ouse and the Cam, and the water cannot get out at Denver, levels will rise. The situation is expected to get worse rather than better. We shall be very lucky if some of the other banks do not go.

But there was some luck. Some Neptunes, 18ton amphibious load carriers, were found in a railway sidings at Bluntisham. Abandoned, redundant since the end of the war, they were awaiting disposal as 'war surplus'. They were just what was needed. The Army took charge and on 24 March Operation Neptune began. At Over, some were driven into a gap of about 60 yards, surrounded by tank panels, covered in tarpaulins and gault bags and loaded with ballast, and then the task of pumping out and reclaiming the land began. And it worked. It was a success. Other breaches were stopped in the same way.

And there was still more luck. The situation at Denver, despite Doran's fears, did not worsen. Tides lowered, allowing river water to pass to the sea.

So Operation Fenland began with the pumping out of some 25,000 acres of flooded land. Homes and farms were damaged to the point of collapse and whatever was left was sodden and rat-infested. Livestock had been saved but everything else that made a farm a farm had been ruined or lost. Some would recover. In a matter of weeks some of the land would be raising crops again and what harvest there was in 1947 would be a good one, fenmen would make sure of that, but most farmers faced ruin and many farm workers, who had lost their homes, had no job to go to with the land out of use. As much as 200,000 acres of fenland would not be sown that year. A relief fund was set up, to which the government gave £1mil, and on 27 March the Lord Mayor of London, Sir Bracewell Smith, said in a letter to *The Times* that he had opened a National Distress Fund. There would be some help for those who farmed the fens.

As the waters were harnessed and began to recede, the Duke and Duchess of Gloucester, representing the King, arrived at Bluntisham station on Sunday, 30 March and began a tour of the breaches at Southery, Wissey and Over, tramping through mud to see the grimness of the situation for themselves. They can have seen nothing like it before.

East Anglia is about river and fen but, just as much so, it has always been about the sea. For long a maritime region, since the end of the war it had also become an area where there was space for much-needed, hastily-built housing along a coast cleared of wartime defences but where defences against tide and weather had still to be restored. What happened along the east coast during the night of 31 January 1953 was one of the most immense peacetime disasters ever to strike not only East Anglia but Britain.

A land flood can happen as a silent, almost creeping, invasion. The storm surge never can. It strikes with devastating force and, at least from the days of the *Anglo-Saxon Chronicle*, has happened repeatedly along the North Sea coast. It is as probable today as it has always been and man is as helpless against it.

In January 1953 it began on Thursday, the 29th, when there was a full moon and a spring tide. Those factors meant that there was already a risk of the development of a sea flood. During the 30th, a large, complex depression, which had come across the Atlantic, began to deepen as it moved from the south of Iceland to a position between the Faroe Islands and the northern tip of Scotland.

During that night and into Saturday the islands, the Orkneys, the Hebrides and the Shetlands, were struck by a hurricane of force 12 and above. In the Orkneys, gusts of 125mph were recorded, making meteorological history. They were Britain's highest ever wind speed.

About noon on Saturday the depression intensified and swung southwards into the North Sea and the winds began their destruction. The first roll on-roll off ferry, operating between Stranraer and Larne, the MV *Princess Victoria*, the Fleetwood trawler the *Michael Griffith*, and nearly a third of the Scottish fishing fleet were lost. Scotland was devastated and, as sea water piled high ahead of the advancing gale, the east coast of England prepared for a storm surge to rage down the funnel of the North Sea.

During Saturday morning there was a sudden fall in atmospheric pressure which enabled the sea level to rise and that, aided by the turn of the earth itself, flung waves of colossal height and strength onto the coast to smash or overtop defences. They stormed towards East Anglia.

High tide during the night of Saturday, 31 January to Sunday, 1 February was due at King's Lynn at 7.35pm, at Great Yarmouth at 10.00pm and at Canvey Island at 1.47am, but ahead of it ran a surge to increase and prolong the effect of that high tide. It hurled itself at the East Anglian coast with an intensity no one had experienced before.

The bulge of East Anglia curves to meet storm. The Wash catches and holds it, slamming it against north Norfolk and into the estuary of the Great Ouse. Just after 6.30 on that evening the tide reached 31ft an hour before its predicted high, rising so quickly that the police were still out on the streets of King's Lynn warning of a danger of flooding when a tower of water crashed over a bank near Cut Bridge and the flood was there, pouring through the town's old, narrow streets.

In South Lynn it drowned hundreds of pigs, but one was saved. It was swept through a kitchen window. But that was the night's only mercy. Over 1,500 people were evacuated and fifteen drowned.

At 7.27pm a train left Hunstanton, bound for King's Lynn. It met the crest of a wave and then, as its fireman remembers, 'We went about another hundred yards and saw a big bungalow coming across in front of us and we hit this with the front of the engine. It stopped us dead, which was a good thing, as we found out later that the rails further on had been washed away.' Water rose to the level of the carriage seats, the lights went out, and the train rocked as a wall of water and debris hit it. The train's passengers were safe but they were trapped for six hours.

Forty bungalows had been destroyed in moments between Heacham and Hunstanton, many of them occupied by USAF personnel and families, and sixty-five people drowned. Hunstanton Town Hall was turned into a morgue. Today, nearby, a memorial commemorates the tragedy.

Sea banks were breached at Wells and part of the town, including the railway station, was overwhelmed as the tidal surge continued its sweep south. At about 8 o'clock it was storming through dunes at Sea Palling to wash away homes, a cafe, a general store, a bakery and a public house. They went, it was said, 'like a pack of cards'. Some residents fled to the roofs of their homes, but seven people, including three children, died.

At Yarmouth the sea topped the harbour and a defensive wall to flood homes and properties 10ft deep. Rescues were carried out by boat, ladders reaching those marooned on upper floors. The signalman at Southtown spent 21 hours in his box before a boat reached him. Ten people died.

As the surge reached Suffolk, Lowestoft had reason to be smug. Defensive works had been neglected in many places during the war and money was still short, but Lowestoft had just spent a great deal of money on a new sea wall. It held and certainly prevented the town suffering serious damage and loss of life, but still parts of the town flooded and rescues had to be made. And there was disaster of another kind for the town. At sea the Lowestoft trawler, the *Guava*, was lost with all hands.

Many places along the east coast were, and of course still are, holiday resorts and although it was so early in the year some vacation bungalows at Southwold were occupied. They were flooded and several people drowned. Further south there was serious flooding at Dunwich and Aldeburgh and, shortly before midnight, high water reached the tidal rivers of Suffolk and Essex.

The Orwell burst its banks over a 2 mile stretch from Felixstowe Ferry to Landguard Point and thirty-nine people died as the flood hit an estate of prefabs – the post-war answer to a housing shortage – at Lunge Road. They housed those in need and seemed not built to withstand violent weather. But they remained firm enough for twenty-four people to climb onto their roofs and wait for rescue.

One survivor recalls: 'We all huddled on the roof wringing wet. I wondered if the end of the world had come. It seemed to me hours after that a boat came along and took us off. None of us could move, we were frozen solid.'

The tide raged onto the Essex coast and up its estuaries. The most solid of defences stood no chance. By morning they had been breached in 839 places and 119 people had lost their lives.

The earliest high tide in Essex was at Harwich. On 1 February it was due at 1.00am. But a gale with hurricane force gusts had battered the port since late afternoon and people who knew the sea were becoming very anxious. The signs were there that there was extremely bad weather on the way and the harbourmaster raised the alarm when, three hours before high water, the Quay was already awash. The Harwich police were told and within 20 minutes the word had been passed to police all along the Essex coast.

At 10.00pm the tide was 4ft above its expected 1.00am height and was topping the Quay. Just an hour later Harwich was completely cut off by floodwaters and fallen trees. By midnight, surges were storming over the Quay, the Esplanade and the Bathside wall, trapping 1,000 people. At Bathside, water 8ft deep surrounded 237 houses and during the worst of the inundation there eight people died, including twin baby girls, sixteen months old.

At Parkeston Quay, a half mile of railway track was washed away, stranding travellers, and the Harwich stationmaster and his wife, who had been attending a Railway Club function at Parkeston, just managed to escape. But they did not get far. They became marooned in the signal box at Dovercourt where staff from a flooded Dovercourt Bay Station had already taken refuge. Fortunately, the signal box was sturdy. On the nearby Dovercourt promenade rows of beach huts were broken into pieces and the pieces tossed away on the sea.

Great Oakley, Bramble Island, Wrabness, Lawford, Manningtree and Mistley were all flooded. At Holland Haven, the sea wall held, preventing Clacton being cut off. Walton-on-the-Naze was not so lucky. Walton's beach huts followed Dovercourt's, and her houseboats were swept from their moorings and into the town's streets. At Frinton, the promenade was ripped apart, its iron railings twisted into knots a Boy Scout would have been proud of. People died but, beyond doubt, the warning flashed so promptly from Harwich had saved lives.

That was not to be the case at Jaywick, which was to suffer the most total disaster of anywhere along the whole length of the storm-hit coast of East Anglia. The alert had been received and, in the hour after midnight, high tide, a close watch was kept on the sea front. But the flood, the devastation, did not come from the sea front. It came an hour later from the St Osyth marshes to the west. The wind-driven tidal surge stormed into the marshes taking everything in its way with it. Chalets, bungalows and caravans were taken and broken into splinters as it ran on towards Jaywick. A second surge followed the first and in fifteen minutes Jaywick was devastated.

Jaywick Sands, in an area of many makeshift chalets and bungalows, was hit when high tide had passed without incident, other than a little flooding along the sea front. The more than 700 people living there had begun to relax, to think that they had escaped the effects of the storm, when the flood struck. It struck so fast that many were in their beds, and died there. Some chalets were overturned, trapping those inside. Others managed to reach their loft or roof. Some on the roofs became unable to hold on for hour after hour in the freezing, howling storm and, still remembered, are the 'horrible cries as exhausted people fell from their roofs into the water'. Thirty-seven people died at Jaywick Sands.

At Foulness, islanders were stranded for two days. Farmers, marooned in their homes, could only watch their sheep drown, but the local post mistress managed to save herself, her cash and her postage stamps – special issues for the forthcoming coronation of Elizabeth II amongst them.

Southend-on-Sea was one of the worst affected areas. Under 8ft of water were 800 houses, and Peter Pan's Playground, close to the pier. Boats from Southend, including pleasure craft, were amongst those used in rescue work at Canvey Island.

Canvey Island, on the rim of East Anglia but included here as part of coastal Essex caught up in the disaster, was devastated by the 1953 tidal surge and it suffered the greatest number of casualties. The entire 11,500 population of the island was made homeless and fifty-eight people lost their lives.

Connected to Benfleet, on the mainland, by one iron bridge, people in Canvey, like Jaywick, lived in chalets and bungalows. Many of them were flimsy affairs occupied by young families or the elderly. At about half past midnight, with no warning at all, the sea wall went with a roar, followed a few seconds later by the smashing of the wooden homes. People were in the cold, dark wet in their nightclothes, clinging to debris or to each other. Children seemed to sleep in their parents' arms, but it was 'a sleep that knew no waking'. One baby girl floated to safety in her pram, but her young parents drowned.

Next day, the boats which had searched for survivors began to search for the dead, in lofts and trees, wallowing along the streets. They became like funeral barges on the Nile, the bearers of coffins.

By Monday, 2 February, East Anglia had gone. Its familiar curve on the map of England was no more. There was just the sea.

While the Queen visited some of the stricken areas, in the House of Commons the Prime Minister, Winston Churchill, said that a National Flood Distress Fund was to be set up. He promised that, 'Everything in human power will be done and all resources of the nation will be brought into action to assist the flood victims.'

During that day, through all the flooded areas of East Anglia, people and animals were rescued and given care. The dead were recovered. Civil Defence, the Red Cross, the Salvation Army and the WVS set up centres to provide food and clothing and to register the names of the survivors. Notices appeared in local newspapers – REPORT IF YOU ARE SAFE.

The relief fund announced by Churchill raised £5,000,000, but nothing could compensate those who had lost everything, amounting to many billions today. They still lived, but their whole life had been carried away on a tide. Farmers suffered £10,000,000 damage and 170,000 acres of good, fertile land were salted and would take years to recover.

In the aftermath of one of the worst disasters ever to hit Britain, while a national flood warning system was set up for the first time, the countless gaps in coastal defence works had to be quickly repaired and strengthened. In almost all places they had been found to be of no use against a storm surge which could happen again at any time.

And now, well over half a century later, it still could. There is a possibility that no matter how defence works have been, and are still being, strengthened, to fortress levels in some places, they could never be adequate. There will be storm surges and floods. What have developed and improved over the years are the warning systems and the preparedness of East Anglians living close to such a threatening coast. It must be hoped that they are enough.

Each year the Borough Council of King's Lynn and West Norfolk, in conjunction with the Environment Agency, distributes flood warning information to every householder, advice on how to act in times of danger. Other coastal councils do the same. It is necessary, and always will be. The possibility of a repeat of 1953 anywhere along the coast is still there and, so many years later, it seems that the best that anyone can do is to keep handy a few evacuation essentials, and a copy of the advice on what to do in case of flood, in a watertight plastic bag. And to have some sandbags ready.

Three very different flood situations in East Anglia in the twentieth century, each a disaster, but ones which the people have come through with fortitude and resolve and a determination to pay whatever the price may be to remain East Anglians.

Chapter 9

The Big Sausage

HMS *Invincible* foundered on the Haisboro Sands in 1801. She was not the first vessel to do so, although she suffered the greatest loss of life, and she was far from being the last. The sandbank, off the Norfolk coast, remained a constant danger to shipping despite having long been marked by 'a floating light', a lightship. It saved lives but, when the First World War began and Britain was at war with Germany, it was to serve another more sinister purpose, leading to the taking of lives and not their saving.

On the evening of 19 January 1915 'two bright stars moving' were seen approaching the Norfolk coast. They were the navigation lights of two German Zeppelin airships, the L3, commanded by Kapitän-Leutnant Johann Fritz, and the L4 by Kapitän-Leutnant Magnus Freiherr von Platen. A third Zeppelin, the Ll6, with Peter Strasser, the head of the German Naval Airship Division, on board, had developed engine trouble and had been forced to turn back.

The L3 and L4 hovered above the Haisboro Lightship, engines throbbing, before going on to cross a mistily cold coast and begin the first ever air raid on Britain. Disaster in war for the people of Britain, from that night, was to be airborne.

During the war, several lightships off the East Anglian coast would be used as mustering points or location finders by invading airships which perhaps had come from different bases on the coast of mainland Europe. On that occasion, the L3 and 4, both German Navy airships based at Nordholz, crossed the coast together at Happisburgh, and then the L3 followed the coast to Great Yarmouth.

Seeing lights below, Fritz then dropped high explosive and incendiary bombs on the St Peter's Plain area of the town where the residents were out in the street hoping to see a Zeppelin as it passed by. They saw more than that. Martha Taylor, aged seventy-two, and Samuel Smith, a fifty-three-year-old shoemaker, were killed in the blast and others were injured. Every building in the area was damaged and almost every window in every house was broken. One villa, the home of the Scott family, took the brunt, its whole front being blasted away and its furniture wrecked, but Mrs Scott was unharmed inside, as was the baby she was shielding. It is unlikely that many will know their names today, even in Great Yarmouth, but they made history and there is a wall plaque on the rebuilt villa to mark the event. There are also exhibits recalling the event in the town's Time and Tide Museum. Mrs Taylor and Mr Smith were the first ever British fatalities caused by attack from the air.

As Fritz continued to drop bombs, he was pursued by men of the 1/6th (Cyclist) Battalion of the Norfolk Regiment. At the Cycling School at North Walsham they had been trained to become able cyclists and marksmen, wearing shorts because, when they fell off their bikes, which was often, it was cheaper to bandage a knee than to provide a new pair of uniform trousers. It was their job to patrol and defend the coast from the enemy. In the case of the 1/6th, under Colonel Bernard Henry Leathers Prior, that was from Wells to Gorleston. The chasing patrol opened fire on the L3 and it was slightly damaged, but it had no trouble in escaping seawards.

Meanwhile, von Platen, in the L4, went on a magical mystery tour, not quite sure where he was. He just dropped bombs wherever he saw lights below him as he floated over misty Bacton, Cromer, Sheringham, Heacham, Beeston, Snettisham, Thornham, Brancaster, Hunstanton and King's Lynn.

One bomb fell through the tiled roof of a two-storey flint house in a terrace in Whitehall Yard, Wymondham Street, Sheringham. Early bombs were small. They had to be because they were dropped by hand from the Zeppelin's freezing cold, open gondola. Sometimes they bounced off buildings or failed to explode. That one did not go off, which was lucky because it landed beside a baby asleep in a cot.

St Mary's church in Snettisham did not have such a lucky escape. From Sheringham, the L4 had gone on to Heacham, where again a bomb did not explode, but the one at Snettisham did. It blew out the church's windows, including a fine, big east window, before going on to King's Lynn.

With seven bombs still to drop, the L4 circled King's Lynn and most of the seven were dropped on Bentinck Street, where they did explode, demolishing several houses and killing a fifteen-year-old boy, Percy Goate, and a recent war-widow, Maude Gazley.

For that raid on Norfolk both airship commanders and their crews were decorated with the Iron Cross, but it was a fleeting acclaim. Within three weeks, proving the vulnerability of the airship to adverse weather conditions, both the L3 and the L4 were lost in a storm off the Danish coast.

Left behind after that first raid was a Norfolk agog and alarmed. It was five months since Britain's declaration of war on Germany in August 1914 and an airship raid had been expected daily, its non-arrival nerve-wracking. But now war had come to the people of East Anglia in their own homes, homes had been bombed and damaged, there had been injuries and lives had been taken, and the sudden reality had stunned.

The morning after the raid, as clearing up began, there were many eyewitnesses to tell their tale but, perhaps because of the shock, they could not agree on what had taken place. Some were sure that they had seen an aircraft, a bi-plane, and they had seen it dropping bombs. Others were just as certain that the night visitor had been a long-expected Zeppelin.

One crowd, which included the Member of Parliament for King's Lynn, Halcombe Ingleby, had gathered outside St Mary's in Snettisham, where workmen were already boarding up the broken windows, and it was there that one woman had what must have been the last word on the matter:

All I can say is it was the biggest sausage I ever saw in my life.

Several explanations for that five-month delay were in circulation. A buoyant Germany had thought that Zeppelins would not be needed away from the war zones because Britain would be defeated by Christmas. She had not been. Or there may be a chance of peace. That had not happened. And then there was the Kaiser.

Wilhelm II was as bombastically keen on German world domination as his war leaders. Although he was to an extent their pawn he had a voice. And bomb Britain? He was not sure about that. He had known Britain from childhood. He had visited often. It was almost his home from home. His mother was the daughter of Queen Victoria. And how had it come about that he and his cousin, King George V, once boys together, were now facing each other in war? As Willy and Georgie, along with a third cousin, Nicky, Tsar Nicholas II of Russia, they ruled a third of the world. Willy, it was true, wanted an even bigger share. But bomb Britain?

Only gradually, over several months, had he yielded to pressure and it was 9 January 1915 before he finally agreed to the bombing – but with reservations based on the mistaken belief that Zeppelin bombing was accurate. The City of London could only be bombed at weekends, and none of London's historic buildings were to be bombed, and definitely not Buckingham Palace. Perhaps he feared rousing the ghost of his awesome grandmother.

Or had his prevarications been a bluff all along? There may have been some truth in all those reasons for delay but mainly, hidden within the Kaiser's pussyfooting, was the fact that Germany did not have enough Zeppelins or trained crews when Britain had so abruptly declared war, just because he had invaded France and Belgium. The German Navy had one, the L3, and the Army hardly more of their own preferred version of airship, the Schütte-Lanz. It was impossible to make reconnaissance flights over the war fronts in France and to attack Britain.

Championed by Strasser, a drive to build more, bigger and better airships was begun at once, but they hardly made up for the losses. Airships went down in bad weather and up in flames as their gases exploded.

Germany had been developing the airship for more than a decade, with ex-military man Ferdinand Adolf Heinrich Graf von Zeppelin, called by the Kaiser "the greatest German of the century", emerging as the most successful designer, so much so that all airships would come to be known by his name.

Airships had been in commercial use in Germany since 1909 and had carried many passengers without incident, but they had needed adaptation to be of use as war machines. Germany had desperately needed those five months. If she had not, the war might, indeed, have been over by Christmas, with Britain defeated.

Britain was no more prepared than Germany to mount an attack or defence in the air. Winston Churchill believed that she was less so. With the start of the war, most of the Royal Flying Corps had gone to France and the Admiralty had been given short-term responsibility for air defence at home. The few airplanes not taken to France had definitely been 'seconds', with no chance of meeting any Zeppelin challenge.

Until the start of the Great War, Britain's defence, had centred on the Royal Navy, the greatest navy in the world, but, as Churchill believed, it had been an outdated policy. As early as 1912 he had warned in the House of Commons that Germany had 'won a great pre-eminence in air power' and that Britain had no effective response. But a start was made and the RFC and the Royal Naval Air Service were formed.

Germany had gone for aircraft and for the airship. Britain went only for planes, as pioneered by the Wright Brothers, but until 1914 had not really treated their development as a top priority. And then, suddenly, they had become vital and the race was on to produce aircraft and ammunition capable of downing the most sophisticated of the new, advanced airships that Germany was turning out.

So, despite having waited five months for that first air raid to happen, Britain was barely prepared. In a way, East Anglia may have been more prepared, knowing that a first attack would be almost certain to come that way. It had happened before. On occasions in the past when Britain had faced invading forces, from the Romans onwards, East Anglia had been the gateway to the country, the front line. It was the first land mass. It was the nearest point to continental Europe. And, as attack switched from the sea to the air it was within airship range. Its coast was conveniently well-marked by lightships to guide Zeppelins in and it had the easily-distinguished shape of the Wash, useful aids when navigation, especially at night, was still basic.

That raid of 19 January 1915 was to be the first of many that the people of East Anglia would have to endure. Nights of the big sausage had begun.

Three months later, in mid-April, five Zeppelins, the L5,6,7,8 and 9 were over East Anglia, with Peter Strasser aboard the L7 with Oberleutnant Zur See Peterson. Strasser, who was later to be made Führer der Luftschiffe, with a rank of Admiral Second Class, was often told that it was too dangerous for him to take part in raids personally but, wholeheartedly an advocate of airship warfare, he was keen to be with his men and to live their war with them, however risky. In the January raid he had been on board the L6 and had been frustrated when it had been forced to turn back.

On that night in April it was the L5, commanded by Kapitän-Leutnant de R Boecker, which carried out the most telling attack, bombing Henham Hall, near Halesworth, the seat of the Earl and Countess of Stradbroke, then in use as a military hospital, before going on to Lowestoft and Southwold. There were no fatalities, but a great deal of damage was caused to property, especially in Lowestoft, and a new feature appeared in the Suffolk landscape – the bomb crater. They proved to be intriguing attractions.

Two weeks later, at the end of April, a new, advanced German Army airship, equipped with three Maybach engines replacing the one Daimler, giving greater range, speed and height, crossed the Suffolk coast at Felixstowe. The LZ38, commanded by Hauptmann Erich Linnarz, dropped incendiaries on Ipswich and then followed the main road to Bury St Edmunds.

Shortly after midnight, it circled Bury for twenty minutes, passing the town centre and Northgate Street. There was speculation that it was looking for Robert Boby's works, where munitions were made, or for a barracks in the town. As half the town's population was hiding in terror and the other half was out in the streets watching, transfixed, two high explosive bombs and thirty-six incendiaries were dropped.

Fires sprang up across Bury and many properties were hit, damaged or set on fire. The Butter Market suffered the most. The premises of J Day, a bootmaker, were gutted. But there was only one fatality – Mrs Wise's collie dog.

The Bury Free Press the next day, 1 May, wrote of crowds of townspeople 'full of excitement at the first personal introduction to the savage tactics of the cowardly Teuton' and a headline proclaimed ARIEL VISITATION OF THE BABY KILLERS, even though, on that occasion, no Bury baby had lost its life.

Again, as at Lowestoft, much was made of a bomb crater. A bomb had dropped in a field off Newmarket Road, making a crater big enough for fifteen men to climb down into. And someone took their photograph doing it.

Ten days later, the LZ38 was back again over Britain. Linnarz's objective that time was Southend. He ran into coastal gunfire and searchlights, however, and was forced away, but not before he had dropped a calling card reading, 'You English. We have come and we will come again. Kill or cure. German.'

Germany made rapid advances once she was committed to using airships in war, always promoted by the avid Strasser. They flew higher, so high that their freezing crews suffered from altitude sickness. They carried heavier bomb loads, slung beneath them. Gondolas became closed, but still gave little protection. Their enhanced capabilities put them out of the reach of searchlights and anti-aircraft guns while the inferior, low-flying bi-planes of the RFC and the RNAS were still struggling to be in contention.

London, with Willy's stipulations kept in mind if not adhered to, became a main objective, but the airships' route, there and back, was over East Anglia.

On 9 September 1915, three Navy Zeppelins, machine guns armed and bombs in racks beneath them, rendezvoused, as usual, over the Haisboro Lightship shortly before 7.30 in the evening, London bound. Many trawlers had become involved in Admiralty work, as patrol vessels or minesweepers, and, even if still fishing, may have weapons aboard. The crews of two trawlers saw and heard them overhead and fired shots, but they climbed quickly out of range and turned seaward again.

One, the L13, commanded by the most successful pilot in the Zeppelin Arm and very much the handsome pin-up boy of the service, Kapitän-Leutnant Heinrich Mathy, was soon back.

By 8 o'clock he was over Brancaster. From there he found the Wash, followed the coast and flew over Hunstanton, where he hovered to check his position. A large part of Mathy's success was because he was such a whizz at navigation when most pilots regularly got lost. He then passed between King's Lynn and Terrington St Clements, near Wiggenhall St Germans, and began to follow the Great Ouse.

He was at Downham Market at 9 o'clock and then, instead of continuing to follow the Ouse to Ely, which would put him well on the way to London, his navigational skills let him down and he mistakenly followed the Bedford Level.

He knew that he had gone wrong as he reached Sutton. Most of the people in the village, hearing the drone of Zeppelin engines overhead, took to the streets and, gazing upwards, had the chill and the thrill of their otherwise uneventful Fenland lives. As they wondered if death and destruction could be only moments away, brought by that menacing balloon above them, Mathy suddenly lit up the scene with the brilliance of a flare. Sutton had seen nothing like it, the pin-up boy himself haloed in the night sky – and everyone lived to tell the tale.

The flare served its purpose. Mathy got his bearings. He left the Bedford Level to fly towards Haddenham, the Old West River, Denny Abbey, Cottenham, Histon and Cambridge. The looping line of the Thames guided the L13 into the capital to hold Londoners in its thrall. Its bombs were effectively dropped – but not on Buckingham Palace – causing £530,000 of damage, and then Mathy left Britain as he had come, through East Anglia, flying over Norwich and crossing the coast at Great Yarmouth at 2 o'clock in the morning.

In his report Mathy wrote:

Navigation from King's Lynn to London was straightforward because the landscape was completely dark and most of the cities were still lit up. London was still very brightly illuminated and was recognisable from Cambridge.

He did not mention Sutton.

Raids on East Anglia became routine, almost nowhere escaping attack, as Zeppelin production was accelerated and improved while, on most occasions, not one British plane even caught sight of any of the airships. Their time would come against the Zeppelin and the death blows would be delivered in the skies over and off East Anglia, but not just yet.

At the beginning of April 1916 the worst Zeppelin raid on Suffolk took place with Sudbury and Stowmarket bombed by the L14 and L13. And then it was the turn of Bury St Edmunds again. It took the L16 only fifteen minutes to bring destruction and disaster to Bury, killing seven people and injuring many others, including a number of children.

One bomb fell on a cottage in Mill Road, killing thirty-four-year-old Mrs Durball, the wife of a drummer in the Third Suffolk Regiment, and two of her children. Her other three children were injured. Local dignitaries attended their funeral on 6 April, with townspeople and soldiers lining the streets as the cortege passed.

The deaths had happened despite the extra safety precautions that the town had introduced. Repeated raids had made it essential to be prepared. A warning light was dipped as soon as Zeppelins were spotted crossing the coast. Safe places, such as cellars, were kept in readiness, complete with straw palliases and blankets. The Westgate Brewery Fire Brigade was on stand-by. And there was extra vigilance during periods when raids were more likely, in particular during the three nights before and after a new moon.

Correspondents to the *Bury Free Press* also came up with ideas for the security of the people of the town. But some reprimanded them for their excited reactions to raids, such as the person who wrote, in early September 1916:

I think a good deal of the uproar in the streets is due to a kind of who's afraid? attitude. Nevertheless, if these lunatics have not sufficient intelligence to know that sound travels a long way and that Zeppelins have scientific means of collecting and augmenting these earth sounds, then they should be muzzled by the police. The foregoing represents my views, except that I would like to add a ban on match striking and smoking in the streets when Zeppelins are about.

Britain was in dire straits indeed if a Zeppelin could home in on a struck match! But were things as bad as all that? They may have seemed so to the people of Newmarket one still and starry night in April 1916.

On 24 April, Easter Monday, Zeppelin flying weather was good and ten Navy Zeppelins left their hangars in North Germany expecting easy flights. Carrying full bomb loads, six of them were bound for East Anglia and, after crossing the coast, one went on to Lincolnshire while one made for Suffolk and four for various parts of Norfolk.

The L16, commanded by Peterson, parachute-dropped illustrated German newspapers on no doubt grateful recipients as it made its way to Thetford, Norfolk, and then it turned to follow the L21 into Suffolk.

Newmarket was a small market town with a population of about 6,500, many working in horse racing, which the smattering of well-to-do residents, the ones with the few cars that drove along the High Street, were glad was still continuing at the July Course despite the war.

The war had brought troops to increase population numbers. There was a tented basic training camp at the foot of Warren Hill, and airmen of the Royal Flying Corps were billeted in the main grandstand at the Rowley Mile Racecourse. In response, community spirit in the town was strong and fund raising was energetic. There was some form of entertainment every evening with many concerts put on and servicemen often taking part in them. But, as long as the troops were about, the public houses had shorter hours. Their doors closed at 9 o'clock.

And it was at nine that Easter Monday evening that word was received that Zeppelins had crossed the East Anglian coast. Lights were dimmed three times, the warning signal, although the town was not brightly lit and there was a blackout in force. Efforts were being made to keep lighting to a minimum, but probably not to the extent that a match could not be struck.

It was a mild spring evening. Trees had the pale green haze of new leaf and there was a turfy freshness from the Heath. The war seemed far away, somewhere in France, and it was a pleasure to be out and about.

There was a whist drive, and some of the troops were enjoying a last carefree dance before it was their turn to go to the trenches.

The warning signal put everyone on their guard, but no Zeppelin arrived and they relaxed again. It was not Newmarket's turn. The town went to bed and then, in the after midnight quiet and darkness, came the drone of an approaching Zeppelin from the direction of the railway station, then almost in the heart of the town, not far from the Clock Tower, a sound as unmistakable as that of the doodlebug in the Second World War.

In the High Street was the *Rutland Arms Hotel*. Army horses stabled in its yard were, for some reason, set loose in the streets as two Royal Naval Service lorries, also kept in the yard, emerged. One lorry was mounted with a Maxim machine gun and the other with a searchlight.

They went towards the Clock Tower and Bury Road but the first explosion, which came almost at once, came from the opposite end of the High Street, from behind Houldsworth Terrace in Black Bear Lane, where the present Churchill Court flats are. The Zeppelin went on to Regent Street. A second bomb fell in front of the *Wheatsheaf* public house at the bottom of Icewell Hill and a third near the *Five Bells*, in St Mary's Square.

People, instantly roused and alarmed, had rushed outside. That seemed to be the reaction wherever a Zeppelin appeared. They stood, almost mesmerized, looking up into a clear sky, to see the L16 and the flashes lighting the night sky as more bombs were dropped. It was a risky thing to do. According to the *Newmarket Journal* of 11 March 1916, a raid on 5 March, 'somewhere in East Anglia', had caused four sudden deaths from excitement. The *Journal* was always guarded. Places were rarely named, and it did not mention the raid on Newmarket, its own town, at all.

One bomb exploded at Reydon Lodge where a man, watching from the security of a window, was hit by shrapnel and shattered glass. He would later have an arm amputated.

In just a few minutes of crashing detonations sixteen bombs were dropped across the town until the L16 was caught in the mobile searchlight as it flew towards Bury Road, cutting short its bombing spree. And there the only other casualty of the night occurred. A champion four-year-old racehorse, *Coup-de-Main*, was killed in its stable, the only one of Newmarket's many thoroughbreds to be killed by enemy action in the First World War.

More bombs fell in fields as it fled the way that it had come, above the railway line. Its farewell blast was at Chippenham Park and it was last seen over the Haisboro Lightship, heading for home. Peterson left behind a shaken town and some very large craters. When he made out his report he wrote that he had bombed Cambridge.

That night, as Zeppelins had bombed Newmarket and other places in East Anglia, there had been no counter-attack from the air. One plane had gone up from Thetford but it had not even caught sight of the L16. But things were about to change for the better, at last.

The next night, in perfect, cloudless conditions south of the Wash, it was the turn of five German Army airships to carry out a raid, led by Linnarz in one of the latest models, the LZ97. An extensive bombardment took place in Lowestoft, with much damage to property.

Linnarz himself flew over East Anglia and on to the outskirts of London, meeting the usual searchlights and anti-aircraft guns on the way, and then he was attacked by two British aircraft. Breakthrough. The War Office had taken over responsibility for air defence from the Admiralty and twelve new fighter squadrons were being formed. One already in existence was the 39th Defence Squadron of the Royal Flying Corps. Its planes were fitted with a new type of machine gun and the first incendiary and explosive bullets, specially developed for use against the Zeppelin. One of the two aircraft, flown by Lieutenant William Leefe Robinson, actually reached the LZ97, close enough to open fire, and it was forced to climb rapidly to escape. Suddenly there was hope, however slight, that the skies over Britain might be regained.

But not just yet. Norfolk, Suffolk, Cambridgeshire and Essex continued to be targeted in raid after raid. Royal Flying Corps pilots were taking to the air more purposefully from more and more airfields, more able to be operational at night, but all that East Anglians seemed to see overhead were the enemy's airships, arrogant and deadly. Questions became strident. Was there an RFC? What was it doing? Were East Anglians to continue to die? The listening stations all along the east coast were doing their job, giving early warning of a Zeppelin raid, but seemingly for nothing. As Linnarz's dropped note had said, a year before, 'We have come and we will come again.' How right he had been. The freedom of the skies seemed still to be theirs.

The atmosphere was depressed, dismal to match the weather, the pouring rain, on Saturday, 2 September 1916, four months after Leefe Robinson's close encounter. It was just the weather to prevent airships from flying. There would not be a raid. And then a listening station at Hunstanton sent word of a Zeppelin. Hardly had it done so when messages began to be received from other listening stations all along the coast. For the first time a combined force of Army and Navy airships was in the air. It was the biggest raid of the war.

Telephone contact was raised with the Haisboro Lightship. Just before 10 o'clock two Zeppelins were hovering over it. They soon became seven. The seven then flew on over the coast, over the guns which had been rushed to Bacton, guns which, in the rain and low cloud, could not even see them.

Zeppelins were, by then, being heard, if not seen, everywhere – Southend, Mundesley, Wells, Bacton, Cromer, around the Wash and all the way up to Skegness. And there were still more crossing the North Sea. They fanned out over East Anglia, some heading for London, and widespread bombing began.

Twenty-one-year-old Leefe Robinson, a dashing young blade typical of early fliers, had been angered and exasperated by his brief, abortive tussle with Linnarz in April. He took off from his RFC station at Sutton's Farm, near Hornchurch, in his BE2C and flew south. He was over Woolwich when he spotted a lone airship. It was a Shütte-Lanz, one of twenty developed by Professor Johann Shütte and Doctor Karl Lanz and one of ten operated by the German Army. It had crossed East Anglia between Chelmsford and Colchester and had then flown over Saffron Walden. From Royston it had followed the Great Northern railway to London.

Leefe Robinson closed on it and, that time, his explosive bullets did what they were supposed to do. He hit the SLX1 and sent it plummeting in flames. A spectacular blaze lit up London, and far beyond. East Anglia felt the glow and basked in its heartening warmth. An airship had been destroyed in the sky over Britain. They had been hit before and damaged. One had ditched in the Knock Deep, off Margate. But the significance of that shooting-down of the SLX1 was the immeasurable boost that it gave to public morale.

Perhaps that was reward enough for Leefe Robinson, it was what the nation had needed, but he also received a Victoria Cross from King George V.

Almost fanatically, Peter Strasser had plugged the use of the Zeppelin, overruling objections that their cost was too much for the rewards, but that loss was a sign that could not be ignored. The time of the Zeppelin was almost over and gradually, from February 1917, Germany began to opt for long-range bombers.

While the bombers began to overfly East Anglia to hit London and more distant targets, the region still continued to have nightly Zeppelin visits. But the RFC and the RNAS, quickly going from strength to strength, began to pick them off at will with their improved flying machines and fire power. Strasser's Zeppelin had almost had its day, but it was still there, as daunting as any big sausage could be but a lot more likely to be a banger.

On 17 June 1917, the L48, commanded by Kapitän-Leutnant Eicher, came in over Orfordness before passing Wickham Market and Woodbridge. Bombs were dropped around Martlesham and then, at 1.00am, flying low because of engine trouble, it was caught in searchlights south of Harwich and came under fire from a pursuing aircraft.

In flames, it dropped into a field at Holly Tree Farm, near Theberton, Suffolk, its skeletal remains seeming to mark the end of the Zeppelin nightmare. It was the last Zeppelin to be shot down over British soil. Almost the last of all.

Still Strasser persisted, refusing to accept that the end was near. His airships were being hit like ducks in a fairground shooting gallery, the glamorous Mathy amongst those to die for the cause of German domination, but Strasser only ordered more raids on Britain through into 1918, until, with summer at its height, the war all but over, Germany almost defeated, he ordered the last Zeppelin raid of all.

On the night of 5 August 1918, four years after the declaration of war, three Zeppelins were seen flying in a V formation off the coast, northeast of Yarmouth. When they came under fire from a Great Yarmouth based plane flown by Flight-Lieutenant Egbert Cadbury two of them disappeared into the darkness over the sea. The third, the newly-commissioned L70, was shot down, spiralling down into the sea in flames. And that was it. After so much death and destruction had been brought to East Anglia that was the last Zeppelin. It was the end.

It was the end in more ways than one. From the earliest days of the first raids, in January 1915, Strasser had been warned that it was too dangerous for him to take part in raids, but he had refused to be deterred. Perhaps he had known that his luck would last until the end. He died in the L70.

East Anglia had been in the forefront of the first aerial invasion of Britain from first to last, beginning to end, and had survived a new kind of warfare, a new kind of disaster, and she had been involved in the birth of a fitting successor to the Royal Navy as defender of home territory – the future Royal Air Force.

Chapter 10

Mine!

There had been explosive devices placed in the sea to destroy enemy vessels for centuries. In various forms, from the fourteenth century in China onwards, they had lain in wait, on or below the surface of the sea, until triggered by contact with a passing vessel. Elizabeth I and Charles I both saw their use in their navies, and they were used against the British in the American War of Independence.

But, in the Great War of 1914-1918 and in the Second World War, the mining of vessels reached new heights in East Anglian home waters.

Always it had been East Anglia's misfortune to be separated from an aggressor in continental Europe by only a narrow strip of water – the North Sea. The enemy had attacked her shores and, on most occasions, had occupied the land. But that had long been in the past. Britain's necessity as an island nation to defend herself had led in recent centuries to the development of a strong navy and in the early twentieth century only an expansionist Germany challenged its supremacy. East Anglia found herself again facing a foe.

Adding to her vulnerability, just off the coast lay one of the busiest and most vital shipping lanes in the world. The lifeblood of Britain flowed in those salt waters and whoever controlled them, from the Humber to the Thames Estuary and London, controlled the day to day survival of her people and the continuation of international trade.

Responsibility for the maintenance of that control in both wars centred on the ports of East Anglia, and Great Yarmouth, Lowestoft and Harwich in particular, and in all of them it became very much a battle against the sea mine.

In the First World War convoy routes and entrances to harbours were mined by the German navy, mines then usually being moored to float just below the surface of the sea until contact was made. In great numbers they took their toll in the North Sea during the war and they remained a hazard for years beyond the Armistice of 1918.

Germany had begun at once. Early on a sunny morning, 5 August 1914, the first day after the declaration of war between Great Britain and Germany, the cruisers *Arethusa*, *Aurora*, *Fearless* and *Undaunted* sailed out of Harwich, led by HMS *Amphion*, to join the destroyers *Lancer*, *Landrail*, *Lark* and *Linnet*.

Out beyond the Galloper Lightship the opening fire of the war was exchanged between the two great navies, but already, within so few hours of the war beginning, the German minelayer, *Koningen Luise*, had been at work in those waters, the first vessel to lay the first of the many mines of the Great War. She became caught up in the crossfire before she could retreat and, by the end of the morning, she had been badly hit and was sinking.

Shortly after 2 o'clock in the afternoon her crew began to jump overboard and, only minutes later, she turned on her side and went down. Of the *Koningen Luise*'s crew of 100, forty-three were picked up by Harwich vessels. HMS *Amphion* took twenty on board, thankful men who had just finished sowing mines in the sea around them. And, as the next day dawned, the *Amphion* struck one of the mines.

Every sailor on the forward mess deck was killed, including eighteen of the Germans who had been so overjoyed to be plucked from the sea. The mine, besides being deadly, is indiscriminate. Ally, enemy, claimer of neutrality, it will kill them all.

The commander of the *Amphion*, Captain Fox, and four of his officers, were badly wounded, as was the *Amphion* herself. Holed and on fire, she was doomed. Calmly, all on board who were able to do so, assembled. The order was given to abandon ship. The boats were lowered and the *Amphion* was left to burn.

From the safety of HMS *Lark*, the destroyer which had taken them on board, the crews of the *Amphion* and the *Koningen Luise* watched her last moments. And then, compounding the disaster, as the fire spread it reached the ship's ordnance. When that happened, what was left of the *Amphion* exploded with the violence of a volcanic eruption, sending lethal debris, burning shells, far, high and wide. One exploding shell fell on the *Lark* and two men from the *Amphion* and one from the *Koningen Luise* were killed.

So, the First World War began as it would go on with deaths from mines just a few miles off the East Anglian coast in a North Sea where the weather alone was often enough to cope with without that added horror.

From that first loss of the *Amphion*, losses of vessels and men sailing out of the ports of Norfolk, Suffolk and Essex would continue as long as the war lasted, most of them the victims of U-boats or mines. Merchant or Royal Navy ships, fishing trawlers and drifters, all would be in danger.

Every port along the coast had its fishing boats, from one or two to fleets of hundreds. On the day that war was declared, many of those steam trawlers and drifters, over 200 from Lowestoft alone, were on or beyond the North Sea fishing grounds at the height of the lucrative summer herring harvest. They found themselves suddenly on the front line of a war between nations and most of them were about to be given a new, dangerous role to play – catching mines instead of 'silver darlings'.

That first day, while the *Koningen Luise* sowed death, the Admiralty ordered all East Anglian fishing boats back to port. At Lowestoft, a steam trawler was sent out to pass the word to smacks with no wireless contact. Fishing stopped, an essential food supply ended. Later, it would be allowed to resume in a strictly limited way, but it would be a risky business with many smacks from Yarmouth, Lowestoft and elsewhere sunk by torpedoes and bombs as well as mines.

But for some 150 trawlers and drifters fishing for mines began at once. Long before the start of the war it had been realised that, if and when war came, sea mines would be used in quantity and that, in the North Sea especially, minesweepers would be needed to keep the sea lanes open. North Sea trawlers, their skippers and crews, able to stay at sea in all weathers, were, as early as 1907, recognised as being ideal for minesweeping service.

In 1911, agreement on the conversion of vessels to minesweepers was reached between the Admiralty and some of the smack owners and a new Trawler Section of the Royal Naval Reserve was formed for their crews. A list was drawn up of vessels which would be needed as soon as war began and when it did, in 1914, 146 names were on it.

They became the first minesweepers, but more would be needed and vessels were requisitioned from ports all along the east coast. In all, over 3,000 would be requisitioned during the war, bringing heightened dangers to an already perilous job and a constant dread to those ashore awaiting the return of a husband or son. The coast's ports lost 214 trawlers, and their crews with them.

Trawlers and drifters still fishing were also likely to strike a mine, and the risk of doing so would remain off the East Anglian coast long after the end of the war. While fishing, 672 trawlers and drifters and 416 of their crews were lost. A high price to pay for a piece of fish on Britain's tables. The East Anglian fishing industry served the country well, and would do so again in the Second World War.

As soon as the Second World War began, on 3 September 1939, so did what was to become the biggest mine offensive in history. And most of it took place in that strip of water off East Anglia, with many of the consequent disasters visible from its shores.

Losses began within days. On 10 September, after only one week of war, the SS *Magdapur* was sunk off Aldeburgh in the first sinking of the war, the Aldeburgh lifeboat, the *Abdy Beauclerk*, rescuing seventy-four of her crew. And, more than that, it was a mystery sinking.

Trawlers had been recalled at the end of August and the Admiralty had bought some and requisitioned others. Through the war, 816 English and Welsh trawlers and 200 steam drifters would be taken over by the Admiralty and, as in the First World War, would be used as patrol vessels and minesweepers.

The sea had already been swept where the *Magdapur* was sunk and yet, strangely, it seemed certain that she had been mined. Twelve more baffling sinkings of merchant ships followed in September and October, most of them blown apart amidships and all in areas swept clear of mines. Before each of the sinkings no mines had been seen and no vessel was known to have made direct contact with one. So – could they have been mined?

It was a mystery, and more vessels were being blown up each day and night. They broke in half, they stood on their heads or their tails, and they went down. Within a few weeks the sea off East Anglia, and especially off Harwich, was a graveyard of ships, their tombstones the funnels, masts and pieces of superstructure left visible in the shallow waters.

Mines were the only possibility, yet none of what was taking place was typical of mining incidents. And then came a staggering thought. Germany must have developed and put into operation an entirely new and highly effective kind of maritime weapon, a new kind of mine. Immediately, the race was on to find out exactly what it was.

The use of a sophisticated new mine in the first weeks of the war caught the Royal Navy completely by surprise and the conventional minesweepers, still, as in the First World War, including many converted trawlers, seemed of little use against it. There were the old-style of mines, and the shipping lanes would be swept clear of them, and then just a short time later there would be an explosion, bang in the middle of the lane and another vessel would go down.

In the last months of 1939 and into 1940, 155 ships were sunk in the coastal waters of the Nore, the command in which Yarmouth, Lowestoft and Harwich were located, as mines detonated in disaster after disaster.

What the Royal Navy, still at sixes and sevens over the whole thing, needed was an unexploded mine in its possession. An aggressive Winston Churchill, First Lord of the Admiralty, recently returned to Cabinet office after several years of political isolation while his warnings about the threat of Nazi Germany were disregarded, was in there with both feet. He ordered that one must be found as soon as possible, and the Navy was desperate to oblige him. Minesweepers were asked to look out for one and, as an added incentive, were told that anyone finding one intact would have a £5,000 reward. Crews, especially at Harwich, became very keen to have that £5,000 and made repeated searches but, fortunately, they did not find one. Had they thought it through perhaps they would have realised that, if they had found one, they may not have been alive to spend the reward.

Disasters continued into November. In the first few days of the month fifteen merchant ships and two destroyers were lost and a cruiser and a battleship were damaged. Nazi propaganda began to boast of the new "secret weapon" which had the Royal Navy beaten.

Still the sinkings increased, until it seemed that all merchant traffic would have to stop, essential as it was, and then, on 23 November, as Harwich was facing its most grievous losses, two unexploded mines were found at low tide on mud flats in the Thames Estuary, near Southend.

Experts were already speculating whether the new mines could be detecting ships by magnetic sensors and detonating at a distance. There would be no need for contact. The resulting shock wave of the explosion would cause the damage and, in most cases, the destruction of the vessel.

It had taken the Navy two and a half months to come to that conclusion when the idea of a magnetic mine may have been considered much earlier. Mines triggered by a ship's magnetic field had been used by the Royal Navy in 1918, but sowing them had not been easy and, lacking sufficient defence expenditure, they had not been developed in later years. It was known that it was possible that Germany may have done so but, without the necessary finance, there had not even been research to find counter-measures.

Sir Arthur Harris, Marshall of the Royal Air Force, claims in his memoirs, *Bomber Offensive*, that some years before the war he had designed a magnetic mine and had pointed out to Government that the possession of a similar device by the Germans would be a great disadvantage to Britain unless counter-measures were in place. He had been ignored and, as the German mine offensive began so tellingly, Britain had neither a magnetic mine nor any defence against them. Despite knowing of the possibility that the new mines may be magnetic the Admiralty had seemed stunned by events and reaction had been slow.

But Britain was not entirely inactive regarding mines. A Royal Naval shore establishment, HMS *Vernon*, where torpedo and mine experts carried out research, had been set up at Portsmouth. Boffins from *Vernon* were at once on their way to the Thames Estuary.

If the long, cylindrical mines found, so unlike the round, horned, contact mine, were magnetic then any metal except brass may cause them to detonate. Before going near the ones on the mud flats everyone had to remove all metal from their persons. Brass disarming tools were hastily made and an examination began. And all suspicions were proved right. Hitler's secret weapon was built around a type of magnetic mechanism which, resting on the seabed, triggered detonation as a metal ship's hull passed overhead.

Work began at once on effective counter-measures which, as the war progressed, would reduce the number of vessels sunk off East Anglia down to single figures by 1944. Many ships and lives would eventually be saved, but it would be a mammoth task, one of the most important in the entire war. As Churchill wrote in his *The Second World War*, 'a significant proportion of our whole war effort had to be devoted to combating the mine'.

But all of that was far too late for three ships at Harwich. The intact magnetic mines had been found on 23 November. Six days earlier, on 18 November, the 8,309 ton Dutch passenger liner, the *Simon Bolivar*, owned by the Royal Netherlands Steamship Company and flying the flag of the neutral Netherlands, was en route from Rotterdam to Tilbury and would then go on to Paramaribo in Dutch Guinea.

Built in 1927, she was a luxury liner carrying mail, general cargo and passengers worldwide, but mainly to the West Indies. She could accommodate 151 first class passengers, 52 second and 32 third, and had a crew of 134.

She stopped at the Sunk, off Ipswich, hoping to pick up a Thames pilot, but when none was available, she continued past Harwich. She had steamed only a few miles and was still in sight of Harwich when, about noon, she was hit by a massive underwater explosion amidships. Severely damaged, she stopped and radioed for help. Hardly had she done so when there was a second explosion beneath the bridge that severed all communications and tore open the liner's hull. At once she began to sink, stern first.

The *Simon Bolivar* went down in a welter of steam and oil from her fractured fuel tanks, and 130 of her passengers and crew went with her, including her master, Captain H Voorspuiy who had been on the bridge with his Third Officer, A P Praamsma.

The water was shallow, about nine fathoms, and her two black funnels with their two white bands could still be seen as she settled on the seabed. Her lifeboats had been lowered after the first explosion. It had not been easy as the ship had begun to go down at a steep angle. The second explosion, when it came, was immediately beneath one of the lifeboats, blasting all those aboard into the oily sea.

And then there came the culminating disaster. The thick layer of black oil covering the sea, where surviving passengers, including children, were struggling to stay afloat, began to burn. Fire made torches of them.

Rescue vessels reached the scene quickly, two from the Royal Navy, a destroyer and a trawler, and a Harwich-bound train ferry. There were survivors, many of them women and children, and 147 were picked up and taken to Parkeston Quay. They included several Dutch nuns and, in their care, two infants black with oil, picked up by the ferry. Others were taken on board London-bound ships. Lifeboats from Walton-on-the-Naze and Clacton circled the wreck all night but found no more survivors.

Reception facilities, run by the Harwich Civil Defence group, were set up at the *Railway Hotel* at Parkeston. It could never have received such bizarre looking guests. When newspaper men arrived it was to see passengers black with oil and to hear for the first time of Hitler's new weapon, the magnetic mine, its existence just revealed to the international press in Copenhagen by the captain of the Danish vessel, SS *Canada*, which had been sunk off the Humber on 3 November.

Amid air raids, operations were performed on the badly wounded and injuries were tended at the Essex County Hospital, Colchester, Harwich and District Hospital, the East Suffolk Hospital, Ipswich, and the HMS *Ganges* naval hospital at Shotley. The distraught were consoled and the oil-covered were cleaned and re-clothed, a local clothing manufacturer providing fresh garments.

During the heartbreak and trauma there were moments when it was possible to smile. They helped everyone to carry on. An oil-plastered patient in a women's ward, the oil removed, was found to be a man. It had been Walter Busby's misfortune to have an effeminate voice and the conclusion reached by the nurses had been a hasty one. And a mother found the child that she had feared lost when a black baby was scrubbed and became white. But no amount of scrubbing could whiten another baby. A West Indian, he was never to be re-united with his mother.

Six more ships were lost off Harwich in the next five days, between Shipwash in the north and Longsand in the south, the first of them a Yugoslav vessel, the *Carica Malica*, going down just north of where the *Simon Bolivar* had been sailing and only half an hour later. The British tanker, *James L Maguire*, was damaged but managed to reach Harwich.

On 21 November, the 12,000 ton Japanese passenger liner, the *Terukuni Maru* of Tokyo, was mined ten miles off the Naze. Unlike the *Simon Bolivar*, she did not go down quickly. Holed, she listed to starboard before capsizing, giving all on board time to safely abandon ship, including an English pilot, W J Mark, just taken on. Hundreds of spectators watched their rescue from Harwich seafront. As she went down she was clearly visible from Landguard Fort at Felixstowe, for centuries the guardian of Harwich and the most vital harbour on the east coast.

Later that evening, at about seven o'clock, two German Heinkels flew low over the harbour, again seen from the Fort. They dropped "objects apparently attached to parachutes", but no one knew what they were and no one, it seems, made a guess.

Three vessels of the First Destroyer Flotilla were making ready to leave Harwich harbour, U-boat hunting. The harbour and its approaches had been meticulously swept and had been declared mine free but, to make sure, Royal Navy planes flew over. Nothing alarming was spotted, so the flotilla set sail shortly before half past nine.

It was less than two and a half hours after the Heinkels had been seen flying over the harbour and when the G-class destroyer, HMS *Gipsy*, was level with Landguard Fort she was blown apart by a massive explosion. She went down in the entrance to the harbour with her bows, severed from her stern, jutting out of the water like an accusing finger. Half of her complement of 150, including her captain, Lieutenant-Commander

Crossley, died. For months after, bodies from the *Gipsy* would be washed ashore.

Predictably, Churchill was outraged. A Royal Navy ship had been lost in harbour. The next day, 22 November, he was at Parkeston in person demanding to know how it had happened. And why, when Heinkels had flown over the harbour and had been seen to drop 'objects', the flotilla had been allowed to leave Harwich as planned just when urgent debate was going on as to how the great number of magnetic mines were being sown with such deadly accuracy, nearly always in the middle of swept channels.

Submarines, U-boats, were known to have been used. The *Magdapur* had been the first ever victim of a magnetic mine. A U-boat, the U-13, had sown that. But there were too many for U-boats to be responsible for all of them and it had been concluded that aircraft, some of them seaplanes, seen so often flying low over shipping lanes, were responsible. If proof were still needed, it could have been provided at Harwich without the loss of the *Gipsy*.

If anyone could get results it was Winston Churchill. He took action. Very smartly the commander of Landguard Fort went elsewhere, perhaps where his failure to fire his AA guns at enemy aircraft parachute dropping objects mesmerizingly before him would not be such a shortcoming. And by the next day, 23 November, the RAF had been motivated to raise its first barrage balloons to protect Harwich harbour.

Six balloons were sited on each side of the River Stour and five more were flown from barges in the river. More would join them later.

Harris became involved. Blenheims of 25 Squadron were used to look for mine-laying seaplanes heading towards the east coast and some of 25 and 601 Squadrons were given the task of strafing their flare paths on the sea.

That was the day that the HMS *Vernon* experts, led by Lieutenant-Commander JGD Ouvry, bravely squelched through the mud with their new brass tools. A few days later the King would award Ouvry the DSO for his work.

Within hours of examination beginning, the details of Hitler's mine, detonated by a magnetic needle which became active when a mass of iron came close, were known and the development of counter-measures could begin.

It had become certain that Heinkels, operating out of Borkum and Sylt, were mining shipping lanes along the east coast and, at the beginning of December, Bomber Command patrols were stepped as the minings increased. Perhaps because of that and the increased defences around Harwich, enemy activity moved north, to the sea off Norfolk. U-boats were in operation as well as planes and the sinkings in that area multiplied.

The minesweeping trawler *Washington* and the merchant ship *Marwick Head* were sunk off Caister, the SS *City of Kobe* near Cross Sand, and the freighters *Onto* and Portelet near Smith's Knoll. Other ships lost were the *Corea* and the *King Egbert*, off Cromer.

Merchant shipping, sailing in fifty vessel convoys seven miles long in recognised lanes, came under constant attack from the Luftwaffe. At the end of 1939 the Luftwaffe was, literally, calling the shots, and if any proof should have still been needed that Heinkels were dropping the mines, that was provided early on 6 December.

It had been bad flying weather, but that had not deterred a minelaying Heinkel. It would have been better for its crew if it had. They got lost. Unaware, they crossed the coast near Cromer at three o'clock in the morning. They then turned back towards the sea, narrowly missing hitting the gas holder at Sheringham before crashing offshore. At low tide the wreckage was found, and when it was examined, empty racks capable of carrying two magnetic mines were found beneath it.

Sixty-eight requisitioned wooden fishing vessels were operating as minesweepers out of Harwich, and sixty from Yarmouth swept the area from Sheringham to the edge of Lowestoft. Crews from the minesweepers, originally RNVR men, had been extended to include non-seafarers as demand increased, and they were trained at the Royal Naval Patrol Service headquarters at HMS *Europa* in Lowestoft, the former Sparrow's Nest leisure and entertainments complex where the popular comedians Elsie and Doris Waters, 'Gert and Daisy', had performed in *Road Show* in the evening and had found, the next morning, that the theatre's seats had been ripped out and the Royal Navy had moved in. A sudden end to the Lowestoft holiday season of 1939. From training there RNPS men went to minesweeping and patrol duties at bases all around the coast of Britain and 2,385 of them would lose their lives. A memorial at the present-day Sparrow's Nest Park lists the names of every one of them.

Meanwhile, only slow progress was being made with those much-needed counter-measures. An early attempt was the Skid, a wooden barge with an electrical coil towed behind a trawler, the first one to be equipped with it being the *Thomas Leeds*, a toughie built to work in frozen Icelandic waters. An electric cable linked the Skid to a 75-kilo-watt generator on the trawler, giving it the magnetic field of a large liner. More, about a hundred, were quickly constructed and put into use. It was a start, but better and more powerful solutions were needed.

Experiments continued, keenly followed by Churchill, who, by the end of 1939, was so certain that an answer to the magnetic mine had been found that on Christmas Day he wrote to the Prime Minister, Neville Chamberlain, telling him that an effective device was 'now nearing completion' and that it 'will be at work in the next ten days'.

Winston Churchill's pet project, the reason for his certainty that the combating of the magnetic mine was 'nearing completion', was the SS *Borde*. As HMS *Borde*, the old 2,000 ton collier was converted into a mine destructor of immense power. She became a giant floating magnet with a vast electromagnet, 60ft long and weighing 600 tons, in her forward coal hold. Diesel driven generators sent pulses of current, alternately of north and south polarity, through the magnet to create a magnetic field of such intensity that mines ahead of her would be exploded.

She went into action early in January 1940 and, after a week, she blew her first mine. Success, but nearly a catastrophe. She blew two mines, and then there was a third. The third one was too close, so close to her that she almost added her name to the list of vessels lost.

When, on that third occasion, her magnet had been switched on metal objects all over her, spanners, screwdrivers, knives and forks, had flown through the air, watch springs had wound themselves into knots, and all the ship's instruments, including her radio and compass, had been permanently damaged.

As the mine had detonated her crew had been thrown violently about and injured. The *Borde* herself was damaged and sprang numerous leaks. She lost the magnet cable, her ability to anchor and all communication with shore. Messages were relayed for her by a minesweeper trawler which came alongside. Like a wounded animal, she limped around in circles all night until, for just the few seconds needed, the North Foreland light was switched on to give her guidance. She made for Chatham and repairs.

Churchill was pleased with her and boyishly enthusiastic about her possibilities. Hopefully having removed his wristwatch before stepping on board, he made an early visit and declared her 'the most valuable ship in the Navy'.

The winter of 1939-40 was particularly severe, with harbours and sea iced, but she was able to carry on with her dramatic work in early February, after extensive repairs. She detonated several mines in the area of the Sunk Lightship, off Harwich, and then swept the harbour approaches, threatening to blow herself to pieces with each detonation. After only a few weeks work she had blown twenty-three mines, saving as many vessels, and on 8 March the *London Gazette* announced the award of the DSO to her captain, Lieutenant-Commander Hudson, and the DSC and DSM to five of her crew, 'for dangerous and successful experimental work dealing with enemy mines'. But by then, poor thing, she needed yet more repairs.

Nine more colliers became mine destructors and managed to blow 600 pound mines without quite blowing themselves. And then the Germans introduced a super mine packed with 1,600 pounds of hexamite explosive. When the ex-collier *Corburn* detonated one, the shock catapulting her onto another vessel, she was blown in half.

The loss of the *Corburn* was in shallow water off the French coast. When the Germans sent divers to examine the wreck the reason for Britain's recent success in combating magnetic mines was discovered and, in response, they began to fit their mines with a delayed action mechanism. Magnetic mines were programmed to detonate beneath their would-be destructors and that was that, an end to Churchill's 'most valuable ship in the Navy'.

Other solutions were needed and two were found. One was the 'degaussing' of all Navy vessels and merchant ships. A cable was fitted round the hull at upper deck level and an electric current was passed through it, neutralising the vessel's magnetism and making her immune. It worked, but the miles of cable needed, if every vessel was to be degaussed, would be prohibitively immense.

The second innovation was an improved magnetic sweep, the Double-L. Two long, heavy, electrified cables were towed, parallel to each other, behind a degaussed minesweeper, emitting strong pulses and generating powerful magnetic fields. Early vessels involved in Double-L work were the Lowestoft drifters *Evening Primrose*, *Sweet Promise*, *John Alfred*, *Sea Holly* and *Renascent*. The *Borde* herself, Churchill's baby, was converted for the purpose.

Intact mines were needed for tests and development by the experts at HMS *Vernon* and a Mine Recovery Flotilla was formed, based at Harwich. Taking part in that work were further Lowestoft drifters –

Fisher Boy, Achievable, Formidable, Lord Cavan, Scotch Thistle, Silver Dawn and *Ray of Hope.* Fishermen of Lowestoft, and their boats, had never been in such danger. The *Silver Dawn* was blown out of the sea as a mine was being defused.

In its final version, the Double-L consisted of two buoyant cables joined together, both with bare electrodes at their ends. A generator sent a current down one cable and across the sea to the other and bang! Another success.

But no matter what solutions HMS *Vernon* came up with and put into practice German mine laying continued undiminished and on most nights enemy planes were in the air close to the East Anglian coast. Many of the air raid alerts at Yarmouth and Lowestoft which were not followed by a raid on the town were caused when mine layers were spotted.

Evidence that they were flying near to the coast was provided late on 30 April 1940. A Heinkel was mining off Harwich when it was seen as it broke through sea mist. AA guns opened fire and it was hit, damaging its tail and rudder. Escaping, it headed for Clacton, but it was in its death throes. It circled the town twice and then went out to sea again. About 11 o'clock it returned to Clacton, losing height, just missing the cliffs on Marine Parade. It barely reached the town's first streets. It hit the chimney of a house and recoiled from the impact before hitting another house in Victoria Road, just off the seafront, flattening it. It tore through several more houses and, at ten minutes past eleven, one of the two 1,500 pound mines it had been carrying exploded making a crater 20ft across and 5ft deep.

The blast in that pleasant residential area, attractive today with its well-kept detached and semi-detached houses and bungalows at the junction of Norfolk Road and Skelmersdale Road, just 200 yards from the sea, shook the town, shattering windows up to half a mile away. The crump of it was heard in Ipswich. Over fifty properties were totally wrecked and 582 were damaged. Of the 162 people injured, thirty-four needed hospital treatment, but only two were killed.

The two killed in the direct impact on their home, Mr and Mrs Frederick Gill, were the first civilian fatalities of the Second World War on the British mainland. Although their house was reduced to rubble their nineteen year old son, William, was found seriously injured but alive in the wreckage.

The four German crew of the plane, all young men in their early twenties, Karl-Heinz Fresen and Hans-Gunther Koch, Hermann

Sodtmann and Hermann Vagts, the pilot, were also killed. When they were buried in Burrsville cemetery just outside the town they had a solemn military funeral, swastika flags covering their coffins, and a large crowd attended, more in sorrow than enmity. Some brought flowers. There was an extra police presence in case of a disturbance, but they were not needed.

A bench at the junction of the two roads now commemorates the incident.

HMS *Vernon* experts were soon on the scene searching through the debris for the second, unexploded mine the Heinkel had been carrying. When it was found it was being used as a seat by the Civil Defence workers clearing the site. They speedily moved from what they had taken to be a hot water cylinder.

Defused and taken to Portsmouth on a lorry for examination, that mine turned out to be the first 'red' mine to come into the possession of the experts and was 'of the utmost importance and an exceptional piece of good luck'.

Red mines had reversed polarity making them able to blow up degaussed vessels. They had been dropped by parachute along the east coast from mid-April. But, as with the first magnetic mines, the experts of HMS *Vernon* would come up with yet another counter-measure. The country, and East Anglia in particular, owed a great debt of gratitude to every boffin there.

The Nore Command, as 1940 ended, had come through the enormous challenge of combating the magnetic mine. Many vessels had been lost, eighty by May of that year, only eight months since the first loss, of the *Magdapur*, but sinkings along the east coast would never be as high again. A small but vital battle in the much bigger conflict between the two nations had not been lost in East Anglia's home waters.

Lieutenant-Commander Crossley and eight of his men from HMS *Gipsy* were buried in the cemetery at St Mary's, Shotley, sloping down to the Orwell estuary, the burial place for generations of Harwich men of the Royal Navy.

Chapter 11

Brief Encounter

Since the early seventeenth century, the reign of James I, Newmarket had been a horseracing town and, over the centuries, its heath and paddocks became some of the best in the world for the breeding, raising and racing of thoroughbreds.

Racing was seen, by some, as a province of the high-bred and wealthy, but in the twentieth century the bloodstock industry was of great importance to the country's economy and it was appreciated that, though curtailed, it should be allowed to continue during a war. It had in the First World War and, in the Second World War, against socialist opposition – Home Secretary Herbert Morrison wanted chickens to be raised, not racehorses – it went on in an abbreviated form, largely due to Churchill's insistence. Winston Churchill, prime minister of a wartime coalition government since May 1940, hearing that Morrison intended to speak against racing's continuation in the House of Commons, sent him a polite note:

> Will you kindly let me know beforehand what you think of saying? If anything were done which threatened to terminate horse racing in time of war, or ruin the bloodstock, it would be necessary that the whole matter should be thrashed out in Cabinet first.

After consideration, Morrison did not speak. On most wartime issues what Churchill wanted happened, and racing continued.

So Newmarket in 1941 was still a racing town. And it was also an RAF town. The two fitted together while they were obliged to but, at times, uneasily.

Just before the declaration of war, without asking the Jockey Club's permission, the Rowley Mile racecourse was requisitioned. The RAF moved in and 99 Squadron was billeted in the grandstand. Wellington bombers used parts of the Heath as an airfield and a section of the ancient Devil's Dyke, a defence work built by Queen Boudicca and her Iceni, was lowered to enable them to take off and land alongside gallops almost as historic.

The Jockey Club, for long racing's governing body and manager of thousands of acres of training grounds and two racecourses was, like Churchill, accustomed to making its own decisions. A proposal that trenches should be dug across the gallops was met with an appalled gasp, and an immediate manoeuvre to put a stop to it. But the Jockey Club played its own important part in the war. It gave up 1,668 acres of its land for military use and a further 200 was given to agriculture. Bloodstock breeding and selling went on, but 3,000 acres of stud land was ploughed or given over to dairy cattle. The Jockey Club itself, a sanctum of the noble and privileged, still stood grandly in Newmarket High Street and, in a way, its determination to carry on as much as possible as usual was reassuring.

There was no Epsom Derby that year. The 1941 Derby was run at Newmarket's second racecourse, the July Course, on 18 June. The weather and the going were good and a crowd of 30,000 converged on the town. Departed jockeys and stable lads may have donned khaki or blue but the ordinary, bob–each–way racegoer was still there. And more than ever in wartime, realised by Churchill, he needed his relaxation and entertainment. It was a morale booster. It was a thumbing of the nose at Hitler.

There had to be a Derby Day.

Racegoers reached Newmarket by any means they could, by bus, on foot, by train and then a long walk from the railway station, down into town and out to the July Course. Despite petrol rationing, they came in 4,000 cars, so many that the London Road was jammed and many people missed the Derby, run at two o'clock.

Possibly the largest crowd ever at the July Course, much smaller than the Rowley Mile, stood rank upon rank on each side of the track, almost where the Wellingtons flew low over the Devil's Dyke, to see Mrs Macdonald-Buchanan's Owen Tudor, ridden by Billy Nevett, win by a length and a half at 25/1, with the favourite, Lambert Simnel, nowhere.

The usual suspects grumbled in the House of Commons about the waste of petrol, but the crowd had enjoyed a day in the sun when other days in their lives were far from sunny. For some it would be their last Derby Day.

And twenty-seven people who had been alive in Newmarket just a few weeks before were no longer alive to cheer Owen Tudor home. On Tuesday, 18 February Newmarket had suffered one of the worst wartime bombing incidents of its kind in East Anglia.

In an area of several airfields, and with a vital road used by military traffic running through it and alongside both racecourses, there had been enemy attacks close to Newmarket, and the Rowley Mile itself had been bombed in a dusk raid on 3 February. But there had been nothing to compare with what had happened in the London blitz and in Coventry. Then everything had changed on that February afternoon. One side of the High Street was flattened in a sudden attack by a solitary German Dornier 17 bomber.

Hit and run daytime raids by a lone bomber had become frequent and expected. Brief encounters with the enemy which could happen at any time of day in an East Anglian seaside street. They were happening at Ipswich docks and the streets around them, in King's Lynn, Sheringham, Cromer, Aldeburgh and Lowestoft and in other towns along the east coast, sometimes more than once in a day. In Great Yarmouth they called raids by one plane 'tip 'n' run' because the bombs were tipped on the town and then the raider was away over the sea. But Newmarket was inland, nowhere near the coast, and no one expected what took place.

A few minutes after three o'clock the Dornier appeared over the Jubilee Clock Tower at the eastern end of the High Street. It was later speculated that the town was not the bomber's target. A long, slow moving, military convoy had just passed through, going towards the east coast, and its lorries had been machine gunned by the Dornier. But, if the convoy had been the intended target, why not bomb it as it was machine gunned, as happened just a few minutes later in the High Street?

Tuesday was, and still is, market day in Newmarket. Stalls now are in a designated market place but, at that time, it was a street market, with a line of stalls on each side of the High Street. Trade was always good and brought extra business to the shops along it. That day the weather was spring-like before a return to light snowfall a few days later and the High Street was even busier than usual, market day regulars from the surrounding villages joining the townspeople.

The air raid siren sounded, but it often did without a raid following. Most people ignored it and went on shopping, chatting, popping into a bank or the Post Office. Farmers were attending a corn market in the yard of the *Bull Hotel*.

And then – there it was. A bomber over the Clock Tower. It flew low and fast, machine gunning as it came, sunlight on the black crosses on its wings and fuselage. People ran for cover. Seconds later that cover was bombed. Many buildings were three or even four-storey, with a shop at ground level and other premises above, a hairdressers, or a dentists, newspaper offices or a gentlemen's club. In little over a minute, eighteen shops and the premises over them were reduced to smoking wrecks and another eight were badly damaged. One shop became an inferno. Three houses were demolished.

Ten high explosive bombs and some incendiaries had been dropped in a line along the north side of the street, the side which had burned once before, in 1683, and smoked out a king. Terrible noise and a hot wind, the smell of blast and burning, black smoke, screaming engines, brick shards flying, people lying in the street, some dead, some with up to sixty fragments of glass in head, face and hands, and beyond, in the buildings, doors blown off their hinges, walls bowing with pressure, collapsing, trapping many in the rubble, some lucky, others, perhaps inches away, unlucky – it all happened in seconds. Many of the shops were old and had cellars. They saved the lives of those who managed to reach them. No building in the entire street escaped shrapnel damaged and every window was broken.

The last two bombs, nine and ten, dropped in front of the King Edward VII Memorial Hall, where a high-level Army officers' conference was taking place, another reason put forward for the attack on Newmarket, and the Doric Cinema, where the sound equipment was being tested. Neither the film, Cary Grant in *My Favourite Wife*, nor the sound, stopped. Both were opposite The Avenue, used by racegoers coming into the High Street from Newmarket railway station, but long before Derby Day, in the first hours after the raid, the craters were filled in and the through road made good.

Newmarket had some high-class shops, especially ones which supplied food and drink to the training establishments and the grander houses in the area. Some, saddlers, britches and racing colour makers, were Newmarket's own. Others were of the well-known chains found in many towns, long gone or still around – Freeman, Hardy and Willis, Hepworths, Home and Colonial, International Stores, Maypole Dairy, Boots.

The fifth bomb had been a direct hit on the Newmarket Post Office, then on the corner of New Cut, across the High Street from the Jockey Club, with its windows bricked up and its glass roof covered with wood. Its telephone exchange often carried important, even royal, messages. It was a busy time and it was there that most of the casualties occurred, with staff and customers killed, selectively. Perhaps it was gambler's luck. A woman being served at the post office counter escaped with only a cut leg while the woman serving her, just a foot or so away, was killed.

Many Newmarket people who were in reserved occupations gave time to the emergency services. Shop assistants served with the fire brigade. Trainers would be on Civil Defence duty all night before riding out on the Heath as dawn came. On that afternoon, Civil Defence rescue parties were on the scene in five minutes. They divided into groups to search the debris for the injured. A first aid centre was set up in the Jockey Club and the injured were laid out in rows in front of the building awaiting transfer to White Lodge Hospital. Ambulances were there in ten minutes, inching through bricks and glass, but there were too few of them, even with the one provided by the Newmarket First Aid Group. Reminiscent of the butcher's van used by the Home Guard in the television comedy series *Dad's Army*, it was a laundry van. It was obvious that there had been deaths, but the living were the priority. Some bodies would lie in the rubble for three days. There would be 27 dead and 248 injured.

A temporary telephone exchange was set up in the Doric, vying with Cary Grant. A surveyor assessed the damage to each building and hundreds of troops helped as demolition and clearing began, sustained by hot food and drink from the Salvation Army and WVS mobile canteens. Rubble, 1,000 tons of it, was moved within two days. But, first of all, the High Street, the vital A11, was cleared. It had reopened in hours.

The dead were taken to a mortuary in a former racing stables, Stratford House, in Old Station Road. In wartime, preparations must be made for every eventuality. Newmarket Urban District Council had set up the mortuary as soon as war had been declared, in September 1939, no doubt hoping that it would never be needed. One body taken there, awaiting identification, was that of a small baby.

It was said after the disaster that the people caught up in it remained calm, with even the injured trying to help others. There was a great spirit and determination to come through as a whole community even if with half a High Street. The Dornier had banked away from the sun after dropping its tenth bomb, turned away from the retaliatory guns and the July Course, had climbed into cloud and was away. So brief an encounter. But already recovery was beginning, a recovery that would make the town fit in every way to stage one of the greatest horse races in the world just a few weeks later. No matter what, as Churchill said, there had to be a Derby Day. And there would always be a Newmarket.

Chapter 12

Baedeker, and All That

On the night of Palm Sunday, 28 March 1942, a night of startling, near-full moonlight, the Baltic port of Lübeck, north of Hamburg, suffered a concentrated attack by British Bomber Command. It was an historic town. In the Middle Ages it had been part of the great North German trading confederation, the Hanseatic League, and its vessels had regularly sailed into King's Lynn, the most sought-after cargo that they brought being Russian beeswax. Buildings from that time, including high warehouses, mainly of timber, still remained in the Old Town. That part of Lübeck, 200 closely-built island acres, was targeted and totally burned, causing 1,000 deaths, in what was the first instance of area annihilation from the air.

Lübeck was a port and said to be a supply centre for the German army, so Sir Arthur 'Bomber' Harris, Commander-in-Chief of Bomber Command and orchestrator of the raid, felt justified. But the focus of the raid had been on the blameless, beautiful Old Town, and it had burned like the blazes.

Harris had taken over Bomber Command on 22 February 1942 when it lacked strength and capability, but it was about to get its first Lancasters. He was an advocate of the saturation bombing of cities but, for that, he would need 1,000 bombers when all that he had in March 1942 was 300. Until he had his 1,000 he would have to select targets to suit his limitations.

He chose Lübeck, sending in 234 aircraft in two waves to drop 144 tons of incendiaries and 160 tons of high explosives, destroying half the town, mainly by fire. He said in his memoirs:

> It was conclusively proved that even the small force I had then could destroy the greater part of a city of secondary importance.

Harris may have considered Lübeck of secondary importance, but

Adolf Hitler did not. He was furious, and at once he wanted reprisal. Germany, like Britain, was short of bombers, but she had enough for the game of tit-for-tat that Hitler decided on. Lübeck had been destroyed so its equivalent in England would be destroyed – again and again.

On 14 April the Luftwaffe was told:

> The Führer has ordered that air warfare against England is to be given a more aggressive stamp. Accordingly, when targets are being selected, preference is to be given to those where attacks are likely to have the greatest possible effect on civilian life. Besides raids on ports and industries, terror attacks of a retaliatory nature are to be carried out against towns other than London.

At a press conference on 27 April, Baron Gustav Braun von Stumm of the Information and Press Division of the German Foreign Office said, in words more revealing than those of Hitler: 'Now, the Luftwaffe will go for every building which is marked with three stars in Baedeker.'

Travel guides had been published by Karl Baedeker before the war, listing places of historic and cultural significance in countries abroad. One for Britain had been published. That intention should not have been mentioned, but it had been, incensing propaganda chief Goebbels, and the international press picked it up at once.

By then, Exeter had been bombed three times and Bath twice, and on the night of the press conference, 27 April, Norwich became the third of five English cathedral cities to be targeted in what became known as the 'Baedeker Blitz.'

Norwich, like Lübeck, had been an important commercial centre in the Middle Ages when it had become the country's second city. The same size as Lübeck, it had also retained many of its medieval buildings as its commerce and industry had developed - and it was in Baedeker.

There had been many raids on Norwich, from July 1940, and eighty-one people had been killed. The Riverside factory of Boulton and Paul Ltd, making airplanes and other vital war equipment, had been a particular objective. But with Germany's too-few bombers needed in other war zones, there had been no serious raids in recent months. Alerts still sounded, but most were false alarms and people had begun to stay in their beds at night and not take to the shelters.

When the sirens sounded at 11.20pm on Monday, 27 April there was no expectation that that night would be any different. At 11.40, one bomber appeared in a fine, moonlit sky. It dropped incendiaries on the City Railway Station and then, as the station burned furiously, it flew away. One bomber. One target. That was all. Nothing to leave home and find shelter for. And then, twenty minutes later, there were three formations of Dorniers, Heinkels and Junkers in the night sky. Over thirty of them. Their targets lit by parachute flares, they flew in low, machine gunning, dropping high explosive bombs. In a little over an hour more than fifty tons of bombs were dropped.

Thousands of houses were hit, 162 people were killed and 600 were injured. Eighty-four had to be dug from the debris of their homes, where sixty-four bodies were recovered. The loss of life was the highest in any raid in East Anglia in the whole of the Second World War.

Thirty-two planes of Fighter Command took to the air from Coltishall, Ludham and Castle Camps, new Mosquitoes of 157 Squadron seeing their first action, but little contact was made. All of the five Baedeker targets, Canterbury and York being the later ones, were within fifty miles of the coast, allowing a quick strike and quick retreat, something East Anglia was only too familiar with.

Norwich burned. So obviously did it burn that press censorship was lifted and newspapers were able to print that it had been bombed. Whole streets of working class terraced houses were demolished and there was damage to the Regal Cinema and Hippodrome Theatre, several city centre shops, Colman's, the Wincarnis Works and the Norwich Union insurance offices. Churches, chapels, schools and public houses were felled like skittles. Gas mains were blown, and the water mains were gone too, leaving fire fighters too little supply. Without water, many fires raged unchecked.

Fire, police, rescue and Civil Defence were at work at once and while the raid was still on, mobile canteens of the YMCA and the Church and the Salvation Army were on the streets. More would be in operation within half an hour of the 'all clear' along with field kitchens to feed the homeless, a difficult task with many food supplies lost in the raid, such as the 8,500 14lb tins of biscuits, gone with the City Station. The next morning, the WVS opened rest centres and canteens and handed out replacement clothing.

That morning, too, queues of the bereaved formed outside City Hall. Deaths were recorded and funerals planned. There would be three burial services, solemnly religious but ghastly occasions at Earlham Road

Cemetery. On 4 May forty-seven were buried in a mass grave, on 5 May forty-two and on 7 May thirty.

As they queued, loudspeaker vans toured the streets reminding wardens and fire guards of their obligation to remain on duty. It was a necessary warning.

Miles of countryside began as soon as the suburbs of Norwich were left behind. Its nearness, all around the city, led to a phenomenon that began after that first night of the Baedeker Blitz.

By 5 o'clock the next afternoon, people in their thousands were leaving Norwich. They used trains and buses, they walked, they pushed prams, handcarts, wheelbarrows and bikes. As the sun was setting at the end of a fine day they made their way out of the city, most of them women and children with a few, carefully-packed possessions. They went to sleep in fields and beneath hedges, anywhere where they could feel safe from the German bombers which had already destroyed 15,000 of their homes. The next morning they would go back to the city.

On that first night, an official report estimated that as many as 40,000 people, a third of the city's population, 'trekked', and they were to go on doing so in all weathers. In some residential areas, 'Whole streets and roads were deserted at nightfall for days and weeks afterwards. It was like living in a ghost town.' Some found a bed for the night with friends or relatives outside the city or in a village rest centre. Some slept in buses. But, for most, the stars were their coverlet.

On the fourth night of trekking, Civil Defence in Wymondham, eight miles from Norwich, reported that at 10.30 that night 250 people had arrived unexpectedly by bus. And what were they to do with them? Other places around Norwich faced similar problems with trekkers, weary mothers, tired and bawling children, hungry babies.

There were men amongst them, many from the neighbourhoods badly hit in that first raid. But they should not have trekked. They had their essential duties in the streets of Norwich. In areas devastated by that first raid as many as half of the fire watchers had left Norwich and they failed to carry out those duties when a second raid came, incendiaries raining down. The loudspeaker vans touring the streets warned them that if they trekked, deserting their posts, they would face prosecution, but some continued to go all the same. Checks were made at night and whole areas were found where no one was fire watching and there was no one to direct the fire brigade.

Ten days after the Baedeker Blitz had begun, men as well as women and children, young and old, were still taking themselves and a blanket out into the fields as the day ended, and whatever they loved went with them. Dogs went, dolls and teddies, a canary in a cage.

The men who stayed at their posts were dedicated and saved many lives and properties, but not always without a grumble. A diarist recorded that her warden was annoyed because so many men had given him their house keys so that he could put out any fire in their home – they were going to sleep in the country. During the raids, two ARP wardens were killed and seven were injured. Nine fire guards lost their lives, all on business premises, five of them in one shelter.

The Luftwaffe did not return the night after the first raid. It was forty-eight hours later, during the night of 29 April, when they came for the second time. Planes circled the city, dropping flares and incendiaries, and then they dived low beneath the fire of AA guns to drop forty-five tons of high explosives, machine gunning the streets as they left.

Norwich, already, was no longer the virtually undefended city that it had been only two nights previously. It had immediately been provided with AA and rocket batteries. Reassuring attempts at defence had been made although, that second night, they made little difference. They were ineffective against the Luftwaffe, as were the Mosquitoes which went up from Castle Camps.

Trekking had left many houses unoccupied, but still sixty-nine people were killed in that second raid and many seriously injured. Damage was extensive, with fires spreading across the city centre as fire guards, the ones who were not elsewhere under a hedge, were forced to take cover.

Stores and cinemas were bombed, as was the Hippodrome again, more tragically. It had managed to stay open during the war and was staging a full variety programme, entertainment, as Churchill maintained, being a morale booster. High on the bill that week was a troupe of performing seals. Star of the act was Buddy, 'the world's greatest comedy sea lion'. He slept in a cage on stage while the married couple who owned the troupe slept in a caravan at the rear of the theatre. When the theatre was hit, Buddy was found, safe and honking, amongst the wreckage. His owners had not been so lucky. They were dead in the Hippodrome's Anderson shelter.

Their coffins were lined up with others, ready for interment in one of the mass graves, when word was received from relatives that they would have had valuables on them. Nobody had looked. There had been too many mangled bodies. Police opened up the coffins - and Buddy was rich. He and his pals could have fish for the rest of their lives. His owner had on him a money belt containing £11,000 and his owner's wife had £600 in bonds stitched into her corset. And she was wearing a diamond ring.

More than the Hippodrome had burned that night. Woolworth's went, Boots, Curl's store, Barker's engineering works, Clark's shoe factory, St Mary's Silk Mills, Buntings. When it reached Cuthbert's print works in Chapelfield it threatened to move on and consume the adjacent Caley's chocolate factory.

Caley's had its own water supply, pumped from a deep well and stored in a rooftop tank. And it had its own fire brigade. As Cuthbert's blazed, Caley's brigade decided to put out the fire before it could spread to Caley's. They tried and tried. But they failed. The print works were gutted while the fire rampaged on and reached Caley's and – there was not a drop of water left for the brigade to fight its own fire. Two six-storey buildings were destroyed, as was 1,000 tons of chocolates which flowed like volcanic lava in the streets.

After that raid, the RAF erected thirty-five barrage balloons in and around the city. All were in position by 2 May, in good time for the third Baedeker raid proper, on 9 May, when, shortly after midnight, forty bombers crossed the coast of Norfolk and headed for Norwich. By then the city was no longer the pushover it had been just a few days before, when the first two raids had taken place. The situation had improved after the first raid and it had again after the second. Barrage balloons, guns and fighter planes met the enemy, defending her in what, otherwise, could have been the worst raid of all, and most of the bombers failed to get through to the city. Bomb loads were dropped south-east of Norwich, at Poringland and Stoke Holy Cross. Only two bombs fell in Norwich – and the Dornier dropping them soon followed them to the ground after flying into a balloon cable and being shot down in flames. If the raid had succeeded, seventy tons of bombs and incendiaries would have flattened Norwich.

It was almost a month, the night of 26 June, before the Luftwaffe returned yet again. In the early hours of a moonlit Saturday morning, when visibility seemed endless, thirty bombers flew in, some of them above 8,000 feet, clear of the barrage balloons, and others at rooftop height. They dropped bombs but, most of all, they dropped incendiaries – over 20,000 in half an hour. It was the biggest firebomb raid in East

Anglia in the Second World War. The fire services were quite unable to deal with the sudden eruption and spread of 663 separate fires across the city. Most could only be left to burn.

Close to the cathedral, 1,000 incendiaries stormed down. Sixty-one landed on its roof and thirty-six more in the adjoining close. It was the first time that the ancient cathedral had been hit during any raid. Of all the historic buildings in Norwich, reason for the raids in the first place, only two, Bishop Hall's Palace, converted into the *Dolphin Inn*, and the Saxon church of St Julian, were bombed. The cathedral was saved when a rope was lowered from the burning roof and pulled up again with a hose attached. The water flowed and eight fires were extinguished.

That night of fire was to be the last until the early hours of 2 August. Then, flares lit up the city shortly after two o'clock and twenty Dorniers dropped bombs and incendiaries. Thirty-eight fires were started around the streets and a 4 ton bomb made a 69ft wide crater in Branford Road. The already burned out Clark's factory was bombed, as were houses in Old Palace Street and Sprowston Road. But it had been a far less severe attack than previous ones, with only five people, including a one week old baby, killed.

Norwich and its people were battered, but they had survived. All the raids had failed in Hitler's original intention, to strike at the city's heart and at the morale of the people. Harris had his 1,000 bombers by then. Cologne had been near-annihilated and his next target would be Dresden, while the bombers over Norwich in one last sortie of all could be counted on the fingers of one hand. Massive RAF bombing destroyed many German cities as beautiful and historic as Lübeck, while the Baedeker Blitz against Exeter, Bath, Canterbury, York and Norwich only weakened the Luftwaffe as a bombing force. Much was given, and taken away, and many lives were lost in a corner of East Anglia, because of a travel guide.

Trekkers, complete with canary, at last returned home to what was left of the homes they had loved, the streets they had grown up in, the old familiar places, and the rebuilding of the city, restoration, recovery, began.

Chapter 13

The Saving of Soham

In August 2002 the small Cambridgeshire town of Soham made the headlines. It was in every newspaper and television news report in Britain and beyond. Two ten-year-old Soham girls disappeared on the evening of 4 August. The search for Jessica Chapman and Holly Wells lasted until 17 August when their bodies were found near RAF Lakenheath, 10 miles from Soham.

With the arrest and conviction of Soham Village College caretaker, Ian Huntley, for their murders, the media and the sensation seekers moved on leaving the town to slowly regain normality.

It was not the first time that it had done so but, in June 1944, wartime reporting restrictions meant that newspapers could only identify it as 'a small market town in Cambridgeshire'. Not until the end of the Second World War would the full story become known.

It began on 31 May at Immingham Docks, near Grimsby, where a goods train of sixty-one wagons was loaded with 500 and 250lb bombs, components and detonators, made in the United States and bound for the USAF at White Colne, Essex, for D-Day use on 6 June.

In the early hours of 1 June its heavy, Austerity class, 2-8-0 engine hauled it slowly and steadily to the Whitemoor marshalling yards at March, Cambridgeshire, at that time one of the largest in Europe. There, the ten leading wagons were detached and, during the $14^1/2$ hours that it remained there, the rest of the train was thoroughly checked and found in order.

The train, 390 yards long, left March just after midnight on Friday 2 June. It was a short run to Ely on a level line. At Ely, 6 miles south-east of Soham, it stopped twice and everything still seemed to be in order.

It went on. Nothing was wrong as it passed the signal box at Ely Dock Junction or the one at Barway Siding, $2^1/4$ miles from Soham, where signalman Cyril King exchanged single line tokens at 1.31am.

A few minutes later, as the train approached the Soham distant signal, its driver, forty-one-year-old Benjamin Gimbert, a family man with a home in March, leaned out of his cab to see flames in a corner of the first wagon behind the tender.

Gimbert later said:

> The flames appeared to be getting all over the bottom of the wagon and seemed to be spreading very rapidly, which seemed to suggest that something very inflammable was alight.

The wagons' loads were covered with tarpaulins but Gimbert knew what they contained. Vast quantities of weapons were moved on Britain's railways at that time and, to the credit of all railwaymen, there were few accidents. There had been two associated with fire. The third, and most serious, was to be at Soham.

Fate had put that particular wagon behind the tender. It was the only one in the train to contain 500lb bombs. Forty-four of them. The only good thing about its position was that it could be uncoupled and driven away in an attempt to prevent the fire's spread and the chain reaction detonation of the entire train. With over five tons of TNT in that first wagon alone there was no doubt that if that happened Soham would cease to exist.

And it had existed for a long time. Saint Felix founded an abbey there in AD630 at a time when it could be reached by ships from the North Sea. That route allowed Danish invaders to sail in and sack the abbey in 870 as a warm-up to doing the same at Ely. It had been the site of a Saxon cathedral in 900 and the present church, St Andrew's, was twelfth century.

Now, amid flat, fertile agricultural land reclaimed from the wet fens, it was producing large amounts of fruit and vegetables, most of it carried by the railway, opened in 1878. Originally Great Eastern, by the time of the Second World War it was LNER, and its freight had become more deadly than carrots.

Soham was a small town. Many a village was bigger. Like other fenland communities, it retained some of the insularity of pre-draining days, relatives living close to relatives, its people content to be in Soham and to stay there. But the war had changed some things. Being 'called up' had taken the younger men and women away and had altered the lives of those who remained, working the land more intensively than ever while

Lancasters flew overhead. And there were crashes close by in the fen – a Wellington, a Halifax, a Flying Fortress.

The war had also brought outsiders into the town and, as if from the silver screen in the small cinema, some of them, from the surrounding airfields, were American. But the sense of community remained strong and it was extended to include them, everyone working together to win the war.

In the hours to come on 2 June 1944 that would be made more than evident.

When he saw the flames, Gimbert sounded his whistle, his only way to alert his guard, Herbert Clarke, at the rear of the long train. The train slowed, carefully. Seeing the fire, Clarke put on his van brake. The train stopped 90 yards short of the platform at Soham station.

Gimbert asked his fireman, James Nightall, to uncouple the burning wagon which, by then, was enveloped in flames. Nightall, a twenty-two-year-old Littleport man, at once jumped from the footplate even though he knew as well as Gimbert the nature of the train's load. Using his coal hammer on the scorching coupling, he had the job done in less than a minute, so quickly that he was back on the footplate while Clarke was still running forward to help him.

Gimbert at once moved off, taking the blazing wagon away from the rest of the train, hoping to reach open countryside before the explosion that was bound to come. He went 140 yards. Frank Bridges, a forty-eight-year-old who had been the signalman at Soham for five years, had left his box and was on the opposite platform, hopefully holding a bucket of water. He and the whole station were aglow with the flames as Gimbert slowed to ask him if the line ahead, up to Fordham, was clear. He knew that a mail train was due.

It was 1.43 and Bridges did not answer. If he had, it would have been to say that he had already closed the line each side of Soham and alerted a railway ganger, William Fuller, living by the station.

It was 1.43, just twelve minutes since the train had passed Cyril King's box at Barway Siding with no sign of a fire and seven since Gimbert had first noticed flames.

At 1.43 the 5 tons of bombs in the burning wagon exploded. Bridges, bucket of water ready, took the full blast. Herbert Clarke, was thrown 27 yards back towards the guard's van he had just left. Benjamin Gimbert was projected 200 yards from his engine. Where the station and track had been there was a crater 16ft deep and 66ft across.

Harry Oliver and his family were asleep in the station master's house when their world fell about them. In one moment of detonation their home for the past 3 years collapsed. Oliver was trapped and suffered concussion but his wife and children were unharmed.

The town that had slept in the sweet hours of that June night was shattered awake. There was no station. No railway. Fifteen houses close to the station were totally destroyed and an adjacent gas works was on fire. Over 150 properties were badly damaged and 761 in a half mile radius had structural damage. Every window in the town and in the surrounding villages was broken. But St Andrew's church, only 700 yards from the blast, got away with a tinkle of stained glass onto pews below.

And there was more luck than that. Due to the selfless actions of four railwaymen there was still a Soham. The rest of the train with its 400 tons of bombs did not explode.

Clarke knew his duties as a guard. Though dazed and concussed, he relit his van lamps and then ran the two miles back to Barway, laying warning detonators as he went. It was only when he staggered up the steps into King's box that he realised Bridges, killed in the explosion, had had time to warn King to close the line. Even if he had not, there had been the blast, heard as far away as Ely, Newmarket and Bury St Edmunds, alerting King to the disaster.

Gimbert, miraculously alive, perhaps shielded by the solidity of his engine which, though derailed, stayed upright with only its cab wrecked, was hurled onto grass by the ruins of the Station Hotel. The power of the detonation had thrown a hefty 18 stone man 200 yards as if he had been a straw in the wind. He was found by railway ganger, William Reed, more concerned for the detached part of the train and the men he had been with than for himself. His main concern was for his mate, young Jim Nightall, but nobody knew what had happened to him. Still desperate to know, he was persuaded into an ambulance and rushed, seriously injured with 32 pieces of glass and shrapnel in his body, to White Lodge Hospital, Newmarket. He was not expected to survive. But he did.

There was bewilderment in the devastated town, a disbelief at what had happened, but quickly the resilience found in fenlanders took over and they began to live through it, strengthened by thanksgiving as they realised that it could have been much worse.

And they did not have to cope alone. Living through a war, there were many groups of people on hand trained and ready to deal with any emergency. Without delay, they were in Soham. The night had hardly begun to lighten towards dawn when they were on the spot, summoned in the first instance by Soham Home Guard.

The NFS put out the fire at the gas works. Rescue and ambulance parties from nearby Fordham, Isleham and Burwell arrived, as did the Red Cross, WVS, and airmen from RAF stations at Snailwell and Newmarket. While five seriously injured people went to hospital, an emergency rest centre, where minor injuries could be treated by two local doctors, was set up in the grammar school. The YMCA served tea in the church hall and mobile canteens providing cooked food came from Cambridge and Over. They would provide more than 1,000 meals.

As the plight of the homeless became known, parcels of clothes began to arrive from Cambridge and, later, from the Lord Mayor of London's Distress Fund. Temporary accommodation was found, mostly with neighbourhood friends and relatives, emergency ration cards were issued and arrangements were made for grants of money where needed.

But, in all, the people of Soham had been fortunate. They had lost their homes and their property, but not their lives. Thirty-five people were injured, few seriously, and not one resident had been killed. The only fatality was a pet canary, overcome by fumes from the burning gas works in his cage in Gas Lane.

As the townspeople, the youngest a six-day-old baby girl, were being cared for by the various organisations and their willing volunteers, the vital work of clearing the disaster scene and reopening the line to traffic began.

With military police keeping guard, repair work got under way before daybreak. A little over three hours after the explosion a breakdown crane arrived from Cambridge to clear the wreckage of the engine and tender. There was no need to clear the wagon. It had disappeared. Only a buffer remained. Shortly after that, 100 United States servicemen came with two bulldozers and set to work clearing the debris, and they were a surprise to some. For one reason in particular they made a lasting impression on the town's young girls, recalled in the 2002 publication *Soham at War*. One remembers:

It was an unforgettable experience, especially seeing the black American servicemen who were working to repair the damage to the railway tracks and fill the enormous hole the explosion had left.

And another:

As we went by the station the next day, there were bulldozers and everything, with enormous jet-black American soldiers driving them; I'd never seen a black man before!

It was an American officer at work in the crater with his men who made a tragic discovery, drawing the attention of local NFS volunteers. One, a young Soham butcher, went down into the crater with him, and there was Jim Nightall. He had been killed instantly when the tender had taken the full blast, and there he was, with his head resting on his arm, as if he had just fallen asleep.

The essential line through Soham, crater filled and flattened and 120ft of new track laid by a team of railwaymen, reopened to traffic at 8.20 that night after a break of just over eighteen hours. When one thinks of the days of stoppage and disruption caused by the smallest amount of maintenance work today the achievement can be appreciated.

By the next day the line was taking passengers, although the ticket office was a mess. There seemed to be only one regretful bystander as the station was so rapidly reconstructed – the station master's wife, Winifred Oliver. With the need for speed in restoring the line, the remains of her home had been bulldozed into the crater without giving her the chance to retrieve so much as a family photograph. She lost everything.

As Soham recovered, the question urgently needing an answer was what had caused the wagon fire. Two weeks after the fire an inquiry was opened under Major GRS Wilson of the Ministry of War Transport.

Tests were made with various inflammable materials and sabotage was ruled out, as was the possibility of an axle generating heat. Examination at March had been too thorough. So what about the wagon itself? It was discovered that it had recently carried sulphur to Luton, but when a wagon was dusted with sulphur it could not be made to ignite. Perhaps a spark from the engine had made its way beneath the tarpaulin cover. But had it? Everything was indecisive.

Ganger William Fuller, called as a witness, had been one of the first to see the burning wagon, called to the scene by Bridges. Although injured in the blast he had remained alert enough to notice a smell 'something like a gas works on fire' – which, of course, there had been. He said that the flames after the explosion had been blue, 'like the flame of a gas ring'. Sulphur burning? Or something else? There seemed no way of knowing for sure, and that was how it had to be left.

The outcome of the inquiry was inconclusive, but it ended with a special announcement by Wilson:

> There is no doubt that the two enginemen acted in accordance with the highest traditions of the Railway Service, and they were successful in preventing an incomparably greater disaster. I am very pleased to report that the George Cross has been awarded to Driver Benjamin Gimbert and posthumously to Fireman James William Nightall.

Many brave railwaymen had been awarded medals, including the George Cross, but that was the only occasion on which two men had received it for the same incident. The citation in the *London Gazette* of 25 July said that they had 'saved the town'.

Gimbert, making a long recovery from his injuries, was able to attend the investiture by the Queen at Buckingham Palace on 10 October. Alice Nightall received the medal for her son. Gimbert's medal can now be seen in March Museum.

Soham survived the war and went on to thrive and grow. The station was later axed, but more houses were built and a Gimbert Road, a Nightall Road and a Frank Bridges Road, appeared. And Soham has continued to remember. Town signs, erected in 1994, fifty years after the event, feature an exploding train. And on 2 June 2007, the sixty-third anniversary of the explosion, a memorial was unveiled by HRH Prince Richard of Gloucester and stands beside the town's War Memorial, perhaps sharing its inscription, 'For Valour'.

Chapter 14

Flight Path

Many East Anglians have flown to and from Stansted, the third London airport. Perhaps not pleasant for some to live beneath one of its flight paths but, for others in the region, handy to have it so close, cutting out the need to journey to either Heathrow or Gatwick.

East Anglia has always been an area of airfields, from the earliest days of flying through to the bases of today. They were vital in both World Wars and the Cold War. Stansted was a wartime airfield, as was Duxford, near Cambridge, now the site of the air wing of the Imperial War Museum.

But other wartime airfields continued in use by British and American air forces, the planes using them becoming larger and faster as the throb of propellers was replaced by the whine of jet engines. Those living near to them, in some cases beneath the planes as they came and went, had to put up with the noise and the nuisance or move away. Hard when some lived in villages they loved, where their families had lived for generations. And, for some, inevitably, there were thoughts of danger.

Planes are at their most vulnerable at take-off and landing. They are flying lower and pilots are carrying out manoeuvres. If something is going to go wrong it is often in the first or the last five minutes of a flight. A person living under a flight path is in greater danger than one who is not, but the odds on anything actually happening are not high. If they were, no one at all would live there. And councils certainly would not choose to build their housing estates there. Or would they?

RAF Wyton, near Huntingdon, was there long before the old London County Council, later the GLC, and Huntingdon District Council began considering the possibility of overspill housing in Huntingdon under the 'expanding towns' scheme. Under the Town Development Act 1952, new life was to be injected into declining country towns and would bring job opportunities and improvements. Huntingdon felt that it would benefit and by the end of 1955 there were plans for 1,000 houses in the town.

The site chosen, which was to be named Oxmoor, was beneath the Wyton flight path, and one for nearby RAF Alconbury.

Work started at the end of June 1960, modelling the development on an American town, Radburn, New Jersey, with lots of green spaces, footpaths, subways and bridges, an innovation at the time, and the first homes were completed in 1961 when the first London families moved in. As the houses were built, the estate growing to house 2,000 families, employers were encouraged to move their firms to the area. There were jobs, there was nearby schooling, the housing was fine, though that innovative layout of terraces in a pseudo-rural setting tended to encourage crime and vandalism, and there were good amenities in Huntingdon and nearby St Ives, but from the start there were the planes overhead. They were an annoyance, an intrusion, and they cast a shadow of fear.

In April 1977 a petition was organised protesting about low-flying aircraft. In the same month Cambridgeshire emergency services carried out an exercise based on an accident happening close to Wyton. That resulted in an expression of 'grave concerns' about the safety of residents in the area.

Emergency services throughout East Anglia were well aware that death might fall from its skies at any time. In the previous ten years there had been more than a dozen crashes involving the area's military aircraft. In the 1970s, up to that April, there had been nine, and two of them had involved Wyton planes. In July 1970 one plane had crashed in Suffolk and on 10 May 1973 the six-man crew of a Victor bomber had died when it had crashed on the Wyton runway.

Almost exactly four years later an English Electric Canberra did not make it so far. It did not quite make the Wyton runway. It came down on the Oxmoor estate.

The morning of Tuesday, 3 May 1977 was like any other on Oxmoor, ordinary lives being lived by ordinary people. But everything changed at 12.15. From that minute nothing would ever be ordinary again.

Canberra PR9, number XH137, of 39 Squadron based at RAF Wyton, took off at 9.31 that morning. Many of the Oxmoor residents had, by then, gone to work or to school. Those still at home were mostly mothers with pre-school children.

Canberra XH137, with Flight-Lieutenants John Armitage and Laurie Davies on board, was to carry out photo-reconnaissance over Scotland before returning to Wyton, with its crew carrying out continuation training as they did so to keep them fully familiar with the plane they were flying. They practised a radar approach and then, in a visual approach on a right-hand circuit, they were to carry out an asymmetric overshoot on Runway 09.

Flight-Lieutenant M Hudson of the Ministry of Defence Air Historical Branch, has supplied the technical information included here. He says that 'there was one major difficulty with flying the Canberra and this was asymmetric flying'. Asymmetric flight meant flying on only one of its two engines, resulting in thrust on only one side. On the Canberra, the engines were farther apart than on other types of aircraft, making it easy for it to become unbalanced. The imbalance could become a roll, which could lead to inversion and a crash.

Flight-Lieutenant Armitage, at the controls of XH137, called Wyton and received permission to begin his simulated asymmetric overshoot. He called again to say that he was on his final approach. All went as it should until the plane reached the point where it was expected to begin to overshoot.

Flight-Lieutenant Hudson explains what happened next:

> Instead of rolling out of the right turn the aircraft banked further to the right, slowly at first and then much faster. The nose dropped and for nearly ten seconds continued rolling in a steep nose down attitude until it crashed almost vertically into the houses.

The houses were in Norfolk Road, Oxmoor.

On the ground, the Canberra had been seen flying normally, preparing for a landing at Wyton, and then suddenly it was spiralling out of control. It hit Norfolk Road but, as if by a miracle, it narrowly missed Sapley Park Primary School, where the lunch bell had just sounded and some of the 250 children had begun to make their way to their homes on the estate, and it missed the houses themselves. Only a wingtip touched one of them.

The crash killed both Armitage and Davies, but the school and the houses were safe. And then the miracle ended. Aviation fuel spewed from the wreckage and ignited. A fireball flashed along, over and into a terrace of houses, numbers 51 to 71. In seconds, they were at the heart of an inferno. Other houses around them and on the opposite side of the road were blasted with the ferocity of the fire, their windows and roof tiles bursting and their guttering melting.

Before the crash, there had been the usual whine overhead. The whine had become a violence of sound and then suddenly there was a fierce burning light. For a few seconds the young mothers at home in the terrace were stunned with shock. Betty Smith of number 61 was in her kitchen. She told reporters: 'I could see flames. I just couldn't move. The flames were coming across the floor and under the table and that must have brought me to my senses and I ran.' Other mothers and children managed to get out of their homes. They had burns but were alive. But not all were so lucky.

Frank Middleton had gone to work as a supervisor with a local firm of magnet producers while his daughters had still been asleep. The night before, he had kissed four-year-old Tracey Louise and two-year-old Kelly Ann as they went to bed. He would not do so again. At 12.15, six-year-old Dean was on his way home for lunch from the school 200 yards away. The girls were playing upstairs and Jeanette Middleton popped into the garden. Dean and Jeanette both looked up to see a Canberra spinning, falling, against a blue sky.

At an inquest in St Ives on Thursday, 5 May the coroner, Mr Philip Davies, heard Jeanette's statement read out by a police constable, PC Gallagher:

> I was at home with Tracey and Kelly. Both Tracey and Kelly were in the front bedroom. I heard an explosion and everything caught fire. I went upstairs and then someone took me out to the back garden. Then some men tried to get them out. Tracey and Kelly did not come downstairs.

Brenda Thompson was at home with her three-year-old daughter, Nicola, and four-month-old son, Adrian, asleep in his cot upstairs. Both she and Nicola suffered shock, cuts and head injuries. PC Gallagher also read her statement:

> At about midday I heard a plane going over. I thought it was low, then all the windows cracked and everywhere came alight with flames. I ran out of the house. I went back into the house to try and get upstairs. Adrian was upstairs. The heat and the flames were too much for me. I have not seen Adrian since.

Heroic attempts were made to save the three children whose cries could be heard. People rushed to the scene from all over the estate, workmen, teachers from the school. Ladders were put up to bedroom windows. Electronics engineer Neville Gayle, who lived in nearby Nene Road, said:

> I could hear mothers screaming about their children trapped inside. I ran across to help. People were running about in a panic so I went into the house. I searched the ground floor of the house but couldn't find anyone so I went upstairs, but it was no good. It was full of smoke.

Fire services were quickly there, but the homes were beyond saving. All that they could do was limit the spread of the fire and douse the wreck of the Canberra and the two bodies it contained.

Air Vice-Marshal Philip Langesen from RAF Bawtry in South Yorkshire, the HQ of Number 1 Group, which included Wyton, was at the scene the next morning. He believed, in what he described as 'a terrible, terrible tragedy', that the crew were heroes. 'Judging by the impact they did their damnedest to get well clear of this area and sacrificed their lives for it. The crew could have opted for safety in a split second by using their ejection seats.' So it had not been a miracle after all. Two young fliers had died for Oxmoor.

There was an immediate inquiry, with Defence Minister Fred Mulley promising MPs in the House of Commons that he would do what he could to have any details not concerning national security made public. Oxmoor residents needed to know what had happened, and they were given summaries of a resulting Air Accident Report. The cause of the crash had indeed been that tricky simulated asymmetrical overshoot on Runway 09 during which pilot Armitage had lost control. It was recommended that aircrew manuals be amended to specify the full drill for the manoeuvre. It also recommended that legislation should be adopted to restrict housing development around military airfields.

Within days of the disaster Huntingdon District Council had demolished the stricken terrace and five funerals had taken place. In St Barnabas Church, Oxmoor, packed for the funerals of the children, Father Liam Crawley said:

> Out of this tragedy good may come. Perhaps this community of

ours will unite into one family. Huntingdon is a very old town and the estate is very new. The RAF has been here ever since there has been an air force. If there had been feelings of resentment and distrust in the past between these communities it is only natural. But now the tragedy has brought us all together. The greatest memorial we could put up in memory of these three little ones and the airmen who died is to remember we are united in tragedy. Perhaps this tragedy will unite us all, and if this is achieved then these children will have achieved more than we could have done in life.

And it seemed that uniting had already begun. Officers from Wyton were there in the congregation and Oxmoor residents attended the simple funeral service for Armitage and Davies at St George's, on the airfield, conducted by Reverend Ian Lambert.

Both airmen were interred in a small cemetery on the St Ives road, near the villages of Houghton and Wyton, where many RAF men had been buried over the years, during and after the Second World War.

As residents of Oxmoor stood at the gravesides with fellow servicemen and relatives of the two men, hearing trumpeters sound the Last Post, they made their own feelings known in a poignant message: 'Oxmoor has no hate, only sympathy, for the grieving at RAF Wyton.'

But heartfelt as the sentiment was, it did not prevent a surge of anger and despair on Oxmoor that after nine years of campaigning against the flight path overhead the accident everyone had been dreading had happened. There had been fear, complaints and petitions, but nothing had been done. Three children had given their lives. The feeling after the crash was that something must be done – now – if people were to go on living there.

Many homes had been damaged and nine families had been made homeless, their lives shattered. Most of them, in temporary accommodation, said that they could never live on Oxmoor again. Others, although they had lost everything, were just glad to be alive.

Raymond Mole, whose home, where he had lived with his wife and six-year-old son Stacey, had been in the middle of the destroyed terrace, said:

All I have got left are the clothes that I am standing up in. All my money in the house, everything has gone. I've got nothing left but I don't care so long as my family is all right.

Within days of the crash the shock and the distress had become an angry backlash. Residents of Oxmoor said that they had been campaigning against the RAF Wyton flight path, and the one to nearby Alconbury, for nine years. The disaster which had happened had been only what they had been afraid of.

Peggy Potter, wife of a Wyton employee, whose home was at the end of the terrace which had been hit and the only one not burned, said: 'I have been expecting this. Dreading it. Every plane that goes over is going to make me feel terrible.'

A neighbour said that she would lie awake in the night, listening to the planes. 'They are too low. You lie there and wait for it to hit you.'

The flying of planes overhead in the days after the crash had been hard to bear, but inevitable. For the RAF, life went on. A spokesman for Wyton said that the layout of the runways was dictated by the prevailing winds. It was impossible to keep their planes away from either Huntingdon or St Ives.

It was too late to go into the rights and wrongs of Oxmoor having been built where it was in the first place. Of the greatest importance at that moment was tomorrow. What of the future?

Huntingdon District Council had at once bulldozed and shovelled away the terrace. In less than a week a spokesman for the council, was able to say:

> It takes £12,000 per house to build such houses, but taking into account demolition costs and other incidentals it seems likely to cost about £15,000 per house. The way we are thinking at the moment we want to rebuild the homes as soon as possible.

A few days later and a step further. One week after the crash the council disclosed that more houses were to be built in the area. Its planning director, said: 'The new development land is directly under the line of the flight path.'

Chapter 15

Step Steady, Gentlemen

East Anglians have always needed to cross the region's many stretches of water between two pieces of dry land, and for centuries, from at least the thirteenth, they have been prepared to pay a ferryman to enable them to do so.

In nineteenth-century Cambridge there were several ferries across the Cam, the larger ones able to take horses and carts, but the favourite with students venturing down river, below the *Pike and Eel*, to watch the boat races in the 1850s, was Mr B Jolley with his fen punt. They called him Charon after the ferryman in Greek mythology who rowed the souls of the dead across the river Styx. 'With his clean blue boat and his hat showing the ribbon of the head of the river he was at once saluted as Charon by a dozen voices and, imploring us to "step steady, gentlemen", soon puts us over on the verge of foundering.'

But on Saturday, 10 June 1905, Whitsuntide and the last day of the May Races, two gentlemen did not step steady. They jumped aboard a heavily-laden ferry, the *Red Grind*, at the *Plough Inn*, Ditton and the ferry capsized, throwing more than twenty people into the river.

The summer for many students at the University of Cambridge can only begin when the exams are over and the May Balls begin. Some enjoy the May Races, 'the bumps', on the Cam, but today they do not hold the whole of Cambridge and district in their thrall as they did just over a century ago.

In Edwardian Cambridge in 1905 the last races were held on the afternoon and evening of that Whit Saturday and thousands lined the towpath and riverside lawns or watched from boats and pleasure craft. Third Trinity was expected to retain the title of Head of the River and there was a holiday atmosphere amongst those assembled to see them do so.

It was a university event and, at that time, there was a conscious divide between Town and Gown with few occasions when the two mixed easily together, but 'the bumping races afforded those outside the university the greatest opportunity of sharing in the pleasure of May Week'. Summer days by the river, the wearing of the finest summer clothes, athletic young men, the cream of the country, straining at the oars, picnic teas, music by the languid stream – what a day it was for Gown and Town.

The pleasure gardens at the *Plough* were popular. Parties could drink, dance or have tea on the lawn as they watched the races. But it all stopped abruptly as the last race ended, just after 6 o'clock, and the ferry started operating again. There was almost a stampede then to cross the Cam and begin the walk back into town along the towpath. Everybody wanted to go at once and it was quite a job for Harry Clayton, taking fares on the ferry, to keep control of the situation even though he pleaded, 'Stand back, please. Not too many on at once.'

The ferry was of an unusual kind, although it was not unique on the shallow, narrow Cam. It was chain operated. There was a windlass on the river bank at the *Plough* which wound the ferry, attached to the chain, across the Cam. The chain was taken up by a second windlass on the opposite bank and the winding was reversed to bring the ferry back to the *Plough*. Operating it was James Skinner.

Both Skinner and Clayton had many years experience working the Red Grind for the landlord of the *Plough*. In 1905 that was Henry Hitchcock, who had been given the tenancy by Bullard's Brewery of Norwich in 1903. He knew nothing of ferries and was happy to leave the running of the *Red Grind* to Skinner and Clayton while he served in the bar.

They had full charge of what a contemporary account described as a construction of wood and iron:

> The base of it is similar to a box. It has a flat keel, which is always submerged in water, and above that is a platform of equal size upon which the passengers stand. These two surfaces are so joined together that the bottom of the boat becomes similar in nature to a shallow box which is, or should be, practically watertight. Above the uppermost surface on either side rises an iron rail or guard fitted on either side with a seat.

The ferry made two crossings. Still a crowd clamoured to board it for its third crossing. Perhaps too many pushed their way on board, more than twenty, and there was at least one bike. It had begun crossing when two young men – were they gentlemen or, more acceptably, 'workmen'? –

jumped onto it from the landing stage at the *Plough*.

It lurched. Already very low in the water, one corner went down, under water. There were shrieks from the ladies, shouts from the men, and instinctively everyone pressed to the other side. The sudden shift in weight caused a bigger lurch. Skinner at once began to wind the ferry back to the bank – and the chain snapped. In an instant the ferry "turned turtle", it flipped, and all the passengers were flung into the Cam.

Rescues began at once. Many spectators' boats were immediately on the scene. Quickly there were 'Ditton men who behaved splendidly, shoved off from spots near at hand in their black fishing boats.' Skinner went out in his boat and it was overturned by grasping hands. While passengers who could do so swam to the bank, eight or nine bystanders dived in. Some of the passengers who had saved themselves re-entered the water to save others. The occasion which had brought town and university together became one in which they combined to help others, causing the *Cambridge Daily News* to remark:

In such circumstances as these compassion unites all hearts and it was not surprising to find that for the nonce the artificial barrier that snobbery or convention erects between Town and Gown was broken.

Fate had drawn many to the *Plough* at Ditton that day, had decided who would have a place on the *Red Grind* on its third fatal crossing. Amongst them were three young women in their twenties, two of them engaged to be married and one a new wife.

Annie Maria Thompson, a twenty-year-old living in Romsey Town was on her way home with John, a labourer, her husband of less than a year. When the ferry capsized John, a strong swimmer, was thrown clear. He looked for his wife and could not see her, but there were so many boats that he thought she must have been taken onto one of them. He swam to the bank. When he could not find her there or on any of the boats he plunged back into the river. He still could not find her. He realised then that she must be trapped in the overturned ferry. With a crowd looking on he dived again and again, distraught and exhausted, unable to leave without his wife. And then suddenly her body rose to the surface and, as women in the crowd fainted, she floated to join him.

Violet Maud Handscomb, a twenty-two-year-old dressmaker of Bishop's Stortford, was in Cambridge to spend the day with her fiancé, Thomas Day, a stone carver in the town. He, too, had swum to the bank as the *Red Grind* capsized and then, not seeing her amongst the rescued, he had gone back into the water again and again until he had found her, entangled in the ferry's guard rail. She was still alive when she was taken out of the water and Dr Graham of Jesus College gave her artificial respiration, which he had already tried without success on Annie Thompson.

When she stirred she was taken into the *Plough Inn*, where Apthorpe Webb, a surgeon who had driven over from Maid's Causeway, saw her and thought that she would recover. Thomas, reassured, went to nearby friends to change into dry clothing and Webb had Violet moved to Mrs Newman's in Ditton for further nursing. She was undressed and wrapped in blankets and hot water bottles. She began to talk to friends and to Thomas and when she fell asleep, about 10 o'clock, Webb left her. But, as she slept, her life ebbed away. When Webb was called back at midnight she was already dead from, he said, shock. But for Thomas the ordeal was not over. As Sunday dawned he had to drive to Bishop's Stortford to tell her parents.

A happy pre-wedding party had taken tea on the lawn at the *Plough* that afternoon. On Whit Monday, twenty-year-old nurse Minnie Eliza Murkin of Grantchester was to marry Swansea man Ebenezer Reece and with them, watching the races, were Eb's sister, Gladys, who was to be chief bridesmaid, his best man, and Minnie's friend from Fordham, Miss Barrett.

When they came to leave, the party became separated in the crush for the ferry. The gentlemen and Gladys got onto the first crossing and then they waited on the towpath for Minnie and her friend to join them. There they witnessed the capsize and Eb saw Minnie trapped in the side rail and dragged down. There was confusion on all sides, there were acts of heroism and rescue, there was so much happening that no one considered if anyone could have gone down with the ferry sure though Eb was that Minnie had.

The county constabulary, on duty along the course, had been on the scene at once. Inspector Sampson of Bottisham, who had seen the accident, had taken charge, but it was some time before he arranged for a drag to be used. It caught in Minnie's hair and she was brought to the surface. Eb, taken back across the Cam to the *Plough*, was so overcome that he was hardly able to stand. His grief was so intense that he staggered about the road, the sweet summer hedges, crying out. Gladys collapsed. As twilight fell, he and Gladys were driven away in each other's arms while Sampson, unsure how many people had been on the *Red Grind*, continued to drag the river. The next day divers would raise the wreck.

A local newspaper, reporting the disaster, called it

> ...a tragedy which for pathos and tear-compelling circumstances plumbs the depths of woe with a completeness that leaves the mind aghast at the inexorable fate which with a merciless crushing blow has shattered the brightest of human hopes and left in its place death and the deepest sorrow and despair.

No reader can have doubted a word of it.

The capsize of the small ferry involved many more people than the two thoughtless, bounding chaps and the three drowned young women. As disasters do, it touched in some way hundreds, perhaps even thousands, of people. From the first affected, as the ferry's passengers were flung into the Cam, to the rescuers, the witnesses, those who tenderly cared for the bodies until claimed, its pall spread deep and far as they were carried away to their homes in Romsey Town, Grantchester and, in a glass hearse, to Bishop's Stortford. In appreciation, the parents of Violet Handscomb 'sent their heartfelt thanks to those many friends at Cambridge and Ditton for their great kindness on the night of the sad event and afterwards'. People, especially in a time of tragedy, are so often kind.

The three flower-bowered funerals, made all the more poignant by the loss of so many tomorrows, brought outpourings of sympathy from the three communities the women had lived in and crowds in their thousands. So many lined Cambridge's Mill Road, where blinds were drawn and shops closed for the procession of Annie Thompson to her interment at Mill Road Cemetery, that police control was needed. At the cemetery dense crowds

> appeared at first to be an idle and unsympathetic one making the funeral an occasion of a vulgar display of curiosity, but the impression was a mistaken one. A deeper motive than curiosity had drawn the people there. Few had dry eyes before all was over.

One wreath on her coffin, alongside that of her husband, was 'almost as much a thank-offering as a sympathetic symbol'. Sent with 'profoundest sympathy', it was from someone, remaining anonymous, who had been on the fatal ferry and had survived.

Flowers, then as now, said so much. Today bunches and bouquets, along with teddies and other cuddly toys, seem to appear within minutes at the scene of a tragedy, a spontaneous human reaction to grief. Then, they came mainly from the family circle and the circle of friends, but the drownings had so shocked that, on that occasion, flowers even came from 'those in a higher social position than the deceased' and from the members of the inquest jury. But no message could have been more affecting than the four words on the flowers from Thomas Day: 'For my sweet Violet.'

Perhaps most of all that ferry disaster at Ditton broke the hearts of those close to Minnie Murkin. Instead of her wedding it was her funeral which took place in the church where she was to have married Ebenezer, her 'dear Eb', before her burial in Grantchester churchyard where, as Rupert Brooke was to write just a few years later, the clock stood at ten to three.

An inquest had been opened and adjourned the day after the disaster. It was resumed under county coroner AJ Lyon at Fen Ditton School on Monday, 19 June, when little attention was paid to the two men, gentlemen or otherwise, said to have jumped aboard and caused the capsize. The focus was on the state of the ferry as witness after witness gave evidence that its box formation which should have been 'practically watertight' had been nothing of the kind. Through the long day it had taken on more and more water and had sunk lower in the water until many had thought it in a dangerous condition. Asked if the ferry would sink, Clayton had answered one worried passenger on the second crossing with, 'She's a good iron-bottomed boat. That wont sink.' An expert witness estimated that it had contained at least a ton of water at the time of the capsize. Other witnesses gave evidence against James Skinner. A number claimed that he had been drunk or, at the least, 'jolly', although most considered that he had been fit to be in charge of the windlass.

So, with Hitchcock having passed responsibility for the boat, recently overhauled by Bullard's, to Skinner and Clayton, it was the two ferrymen who were deemed answerable for the accident and the three deaths. They had made it their duty to carry people over the river and, the coroner told the jury, if they had been negligent in that duty they were criminally responsible and could face charges of manslaughter. They were not to hesitate if that was their verdict.

After only 25 minutes the jury reached its verdict. Accidental death. The ferrymen, it was determined, had mismanaged the boat but had not fully appreciated the responsibility that went with the job. They both were censured and were told that, in future, they should take more care. Step steady, gentlemen.

The life of King's Lynn, from earliest times, centred on the tidal Great Ouse and its outfall into the Wash and the North Sea. There are records of a ferry across the Ouse to West Lynn in 1285, making it one of the earliest in the country. It was used by pilgrims to Walsingham, by the Duke of Clarence and his household in 1413 and, eight years later, by the king, Henry V. A brave man considering that disasters were so frequent that it became the custom to toll the church bells for the drowned.

In 1796 there were twenty-two deaths. Most of them happened on 23 February. A ferry left the Common Staithe, the town's main public quay, to cross the Ouse at seven o'clock in the evening with thirty or more passengers on board. It was overloaded, but no passengers had stepped back onto the quay when the ferryman had asked that some of them wait the few minutes for his return and the next crossing.

It was cold but calm, with a wintry dark settled over the water and a strong tide running. As the ferry neared the far bank, the current took it and it collided with a clay barge and overturned. Twenty of its passengers died but one, John Price, a sailor, managed to rescue four. He tried to save a fifth but the power of the tide swept the woman from his arms, nearly carrying him away with her. Among the drowned were a young couple, about to be married. When their bodies were recovered they were, in death as in life, clasped in each other's arms.

Perhaps the Great Ouse ferryman should have been more raucous in his warning of overloading, more like the old boy at Surlingham where, until the 1940s, a vehicle ferry crossed the Yare between Norwich and Great Yarmouth, who would warn, 'If you really want to go across I'll take you, but the old boat's rotten and I don't know whether we'll get there.'

As the train and then the car made East Anglia a smaller place, they widened the horizons of travellers everywhere. River ferries declined, although the one at Lynn, for pedestrians, still crosses the Ouse, as does a foot and cycle ferry between Harwich and Felixstowe in the summer months. Sights were set on continental Europe, the sea ferry came into existence, and both those places became ferry ports.

From the 1840s, small packet boats crossed the North Sea with a few passengers. Just over a century later, developed from the landing craft used in the Second World War, ferries had become roll-on roll-off, transforming the carriage of vehicles. Large numbers of cars and lorries could be quickly loaded and unloaded using ramps and bow and stern doors, revolutionising the short sea crossing and travel and trade between East Anglia, Scandinavia and mainland Europe.

But the design, with large doors just above the waterline and open vehicle decks without bulkheads, was controversial. If a door was not properly secured and water got onto the deck its movement could cause instability and capsize.

The loss of the first RORO of all, the *Princess Victoria*, in the storm that led to the east coast tidal surge at the end of January 1953, when her stern doors failed, was an omen. Disasters continued. In the decade from 1973 there had been fifteen RORO accidents involving loss of life, three of them linked to Felixstowe, when, as 1982 ended, the *Speedlink Vanguard* met the *European Gateway*.

The headline of the Cambridge Evening News on Monday, 20 December 1982 was one stark black word – COLLISION. That of the *East Anglian Daily Times* told more:

HARWICH RESCUE BID OFF SUFFOLK COAST AS FERRIES COLLIDE.

The weather had been bad on Sunday, 19 December as one of the deepest depressions for many years hit Britain. Winds had been storm force 10 before easing, but they were still a force 6 south westerly gale and bitter. The sea was heavy with a 7ft rise, but visibility was good as the 4,263 ton Townsend Thoresen *European Gateway*, carrying lorries and their drivers, left Felixstowe for Rotterdam in the late evening.

She had sailed only five miles when, in the approaches to the mouth of the Orwell, she was in collision with the *Speedlink Vanguard*, a 3,514 ton Sealink train ferry from Zeebrugge making for Harwich.

Both vessels were in a 1,000 yard wide channel, dredged to a depth of 30ft between sandbanks, and should have been no more than ships that pass in the night. Both were equipped with up-to-date radar and radio and yet both sailed on the same side of the channel and met at an angle to each other. In a massive impact, the bulbous bow of the *Vanguard* hit the *Gateway* amidships, scraping along her starboard side and ripping a hole 200ft long in her hull while sustaining only superficial damage herself. She would make Harwich unaided with none of those on board, twenty-eight crew members and no passengers, injured.

Men in the *Gateway*'s engine room at once saw 'a wall of water' and then, in a matter of seconds, they were inundated. Two of them lost their lives.

ROROs were not only prone to disaster, they were liable to sink quickly once a disaster had occurred. By some they were called roll-on roll-overs. The *Titanic* stayed afloat on an even keel for two and a half hours after being holed by an iceberg. With a RORO it could be less than six minutes. In the case of the *European Gateway* it was about ten minutes before, her decks flooded and, lorries crashing about, breaking free and through her stern door, she rolled over onto her starboard side.

She foundered on a sandbank in 20ft of water off Felixstowe seafront, on the edge of the dredged channel. The collision was reported at 10.48pm, only 18 minutes after she had left Felixstowe. It was to be the Suffolk coast's worst shipping disaster in many years.

On board the *Gateway* were thirty-six crew and thirty-four passengers, most of them British and Dutch lorry drivers. Every man on board raced to save himself in whatever way he could, and some encountered problems. In the next day's newspapers claims were made that lifesaving equipment had been faulty or missing.

Dutch lorry driver, Joop Josee, from Hilversum, said:

> Somebody told me to get a lifebelt but when I went back to my cabin there wasn't one there. I looked everywhere, but there was nothing. Then they couldn't get the lifeboats launched.

Lifeboats had been damaged by the *Vanguard*, or could not be launched because of the listing of the *Gateway*, but some life rafts were put into the sea and men jumped aboard. Others took their chance by leaping into the icy, storm-lashed water. Some men, the non-swimmers amongst them, clung to the parts of the gale-battered hull that remained above water, hoping for a speedy rescue.

No-one realised at the time that they were in water so shallow that the vessel could not sink completely. She would only lie on her side. But, with weather conditions as they were, that was bad enough.

And luck was with the *European Gateway*. Despite the foul conditions, several small boats were close by and they raced to her aid - pilot boats *Patrol* and *Valour*, and the harbour tugs *Ganges*, *Alfred* and *Sauria*.

Time after time, battling the seas and disregarding the dangers, they approached the ferry and saved men, from the sea and from the vessel. The *Valour* in particular, under Coxswain Ken Lee, lived up to her name. She rescued twenty-eight survivors and picked up three dead bodies.

Going alongside, Lee said: "The stern was under when we got there. She had swung across the tide. The lads couldn't get into the lifeboats because they were hanging at an angle because of the list."

After three attempts, backed up by the *Patrol*, the *Valour* managed to nudge a lifeboat closer to the twenty-eight men clinging to the rails of the *Gateway* so that they could use it to reach the pilot boat. Crewman Barry Warner, a Dovercourt man, said:

I was in the afterdeck pulling them on as fast as they could come. As she was going you could hear everything crashing about inside her. All the time I thought she would go. Further astern lorries and containers dropped into the water.

He threw a lifebelt to two men who had lost their grip and fallen into the sea and pulled them to the *Valour*: 'I had to shout to the others for assistance. They just stood there. They were so shocked.' And perhaps afraid. Another crew member admitted, 'I have never been so scared in my life.'

All the boats were involved in the rescue and there was bravery by all men on all of them, down to the youngest man. A seventeen-year-old deckhand, Jason Woodward of Felixstowe, said: 'I was hanging over the side of the tug with my mate hanging on to me holding this bloke's hand.'

Later, Captain Jack Hart, Superintendent of Pilots at Harwich, said of all who had taken part: 'These men showed great courage. If they had not gone back again and again more might have perished.'

The small boats had quickly been joined in the rescue operation by the Harwich and Walton lifeboats, two helicopters from RAF Manston, a Seaking from Belgium and a USAF Chinook, a 'Jolly Green Giant', from RAF Woodbridge. The Danish container ship, the *Dana Futura*, inbound for Parkeston Quay, which had just taken on board a pilot from the *Valour*, closed in to light the scene with her searchlights and to take the rescued aboard, reviving them in the ship's sauna.

All survivors were picked up within an hour of the collision. A remarkable achievement. The search ended when the Harwich lifeboat, the *John Fison*, had been at sea for seven hours and had recovered two bodies. Five men had died, two passengers and three crew members, and one crewman was missing. There had been no serious injuries and the survivors, treated for cold, exposure and shock, would all make a good recovery, thanks to their rescuers at sea, backed up by emergency services on shore. A fund to help relatives of the dead was set up by the Mayor of Felixstowe, Tom Savage.

For their part in the rescue, the crews of the pilot boats were awarded the RNLI Bronze Medal. Framed letters of appreciation were presented to the masters of the tugs and the coxswains and crew of the lifeboats.

The day after the collision, as the body of Joseph Topp, motor man, the missing crew member, was recovered from the Gateway's engine room by Dutch divers, a Board of Trade and Industry Inquiry began. Questions were asked in the House of Commons and several MPs, including Sir Julian Ridsdale for Harwich and Keith Stainton for Sudbury and Woodbridge, called for an investigation. Greater ferry safety was obviously needed. The question of the complaints about the lifesaving equipment was raised, and answered. The *European Gateway*, MPs were assured, had a passenger certificate requiring the provision of a lifejacket and space aboard life rafts for every passenger and crew member. It could not have sailed without them. The main causes for concern were how the two ferries had come to meet in the first place, and why the *Gateway* had so promptly capsized.

The Court of Inquiry into the accident, chaired by the Commissioner of Wrecks, Nicholas Phillips QC, began on 5 November 1983, and was attended by the masters of both vessels, both experienced men with many years of excellent service on ferries in the Irish and North Seas. On 3 August 1984 the Inquiry's ninety-eight page report was published.

In it, both captains were blamed for navigational errors leading to the loss of the £18m *European Gateway* at a time when modern radar provided an alternative to compass bearings as a way of detecting collision risks. The severest criticism was meted out to Herbert McGibney, a Preston man, master of the *Gateway*, who 'failed to keep a good lookout and attempted to cross ahead of the other vessel when it was unsafe to do so'. He was found guilty of 'serious negligence in navigation'. John Bolton, master of the *Vanguard*, was found at fault for 'failing to react correctly in the confusion caused by McGibney'. He initially altered course to starboard without slowing down 'at a time when he should have instead taken off his way'.

Both men, it was said, had previously had 'unblemished and outstanding service records'. Townsend Thoresen thought criticism of its man 'harsh' and, as he was censured, said that it was standing by him. Bolton was admonished, and said that he was 'not entirely happy' about it.

It was said that the *Gateway* capsized on her starboard side in ten minutes as the crew fought to close three watertight doors, still open when the vessel was eighteen minutes out of Felixstowe. They only managed to fully close one and to half-close another. The report said that regulations must be changed enabling passenger vessels to operate more easily with the doors closed, and automatic, powered operation must be mandatory for all ferry doors.

The *Gateway*'s generator, stabiliser and gearbox rooms had all flooded – and the main engine room had been overwhelmed within seconds of the collision. The main deck had flooded from one side, causing the immediate list, the roll over. It was felt essential that "funds should be provided for research into the phenomenon", a phenomenon long appreciated as a shortcoming of the RORO.

The crew were praised for their lack of panic, but the report said that the good order on board during the capsize and subsequent rescue was mainly due to the fact that most of the passengers were long-distance lorry drivers, "men of independent spirit and resource."

Undoubtedly they were, but they had still complained at the inadequacy of lifesaving equipment. The report also dealt with that, recommending that each ferry must have at least two loud hailers for communication and a uniform system of storing lifejackets.

So, one of the most serious sea disasters off Felixstowe in recent years, the loss of a ferry and of six lives, ended with the ferrymen, as on the Cam in 1905, paying the price, although they were both allowed to keep their master's certificate and continued to put to sea.

As a result of the report some structural changes to improve safety were made to ROROs, but not quickly enough for one vessel at least. In March 1987, two and a half years after the publication of the report into the capsize of the *European Gateway*, the *Herald of Free Enterprise* capsized, rolled over in just a few minutes, when her bow cargo door remained open as she left Zeebrugge, a ferry disaster which took the lives of 193 of her passengers.

Select Bibliography

(1) Books and Journals

Bagshaw, Robert *A Norfolk Chronicle*, G R Reeve Ltd, Wymondham, 1997

Baker, Eddie *A History of Firefighting in Cambridgeshire*, Jeremy Mills Publishing, Huddersfield, 2006

Basham, John E Brandon *1789 – a village fire*, Salient Press, Ipswich, 1986

Benham, Hervey *Once Upon a Tide*, George Harrap and Co Ltd, London, 1986

Bowyer, Jack *The Evolution of Church Building*, Granada Publishing, London, 1977

Bowyer, Michael J T *Air Raid!* Patrick Stephens, Wellingborough, 1986

Brown, R Douglas *East Anglia 1942*, Terence Dalton Ltd, Lavenham, 1988

Braun, Hugh *English Abbeys*, Faber and Faber, London, 1971

Brooks, Pamela *Norwich; Stories of a City*, Font Publishing, Ayr, 2003

Brooks, Pamela *The Norfolk Almanac of Disasters*, Breedon Books, Derby, 2007

Chant, Katharine *The History of Dunwich*, Dunwich Museum, 1986

Clay, Catrine *King, Kaiser, Tsar*, John Murray, London, 2006

Clayton, Joseph *Robert Kett and the Norfolk Rising*, Martin Secker, London, 1912

Collier, Basil *A History of Air Power*, Weidenfeld and Nicolson, London, 1974

Day, Anthony *But for Such Men as These*, SB Publications, Seaford, 1994

Day, Anthony *Times of Flood*, SB Publications, Seaford, 1997

Dunn, Chris '*The Tragedy of the Flaming Heart*', Cambridgeshire, May 2005, 88-89

Fairhall, David *East Anglian Shores*, Greenwich Editions, London, 1995

Foynes, JP *The Battle of the East Coast (1939-1945)*, own publication, no date, c1960

Gallyon, Margaret *The Early Church in Eastern England*, Terence Dalton Ltd, Lavenham, 1973

Gerard, Malcolm and Hamilton, JAB *Rails to Disaster*, George Allen and Unwin, London, 1984

Gibbons, Rev Thomas *An Account of a Most Terrible FIRE, Etc*, 1769

Glenn, Alfred *Weather Patterns of East Anglia*, Terence Dalton Ltd, Lavenham, 1987

Green, E Tyrrell *Towers and Spires, Their Design and Arrangement*, Wells Gardner, Danton and Co Ltd, London, 1907

Griehl, Manfred and Dresel, Joachim *Zeppelin!* Arms and Armour Press, London, 1990

Grieve, Hilda *The Great Tide*, Essex County Council, Chelmsford, 1959

Grocott, Terence *Shipwrecks of the Revolutionary and Napoleonic Eras*, Chatham Publishing, London, 1997

Harland, M G and H J *The Flooding of Eastern England*, Minimax Books Ltd, Peterborough, 1980

Harris, Sir Arthur *Bomber Offensive*, L Cooper, London, 2005

Hendy, Phyllis M *Treacherous Tides*, own compilation, 2007

Hussey, Frank *Suffolk Invasion*, Terence Dalton Ltd, Lavenham, 1983

Jarvis, Stan *East Anglia Shipwrecks*, Countryside Books, Newbury, 1990

Johnson, Derek E *East Anglia at War 1939-45*, Jarrold Publishing, Norwich, 1992

Land, Stephen K *Kett's Rebellion: The Norfolk Rising of 1549*, Boydell Press Ltd, Ipswich, 1977

Lund, Paul and Ludham, Harry *Trawlers go to War*, Foulsham and Co, London, 1971

Lund, Paul and Ludham, Harry *Out Sweeps!* Foulsham and Co, London, 1978

Manning, A S *Dunwich: East Anglia's Atlantis*, Arthur H Stockwell Ltd, Ilfracombe, 1995

May, Peter *The Changing Face of Newmarket 1600-1760*, Peter May Publications Ltd, Newmarket, 1984

Meeres, Frank *Norfolk in the Second World War*, Phillimore and Co Ltd, Chichester, 2006

Nock, OS *Historic Railway Disasters*, Ian Allen Ltd, London, 1987

Occomore, Dave (ed) *One Afternoon in February*, Newmarket Local History Society, 2001

Pollard, Michael *North Sea Surge*, Terence Dalton Ltd, Lavenham, 1978

Reeve, Terry *The Day Bungay Burned*, Morrow and Co, Bungay, 1988

Richardson, H *Burwell. A Stroll Through History*, own publication, 1990

Robinson, Robb *Trawling*, University of Exeter Press, Exeter, 1996

Rolt, LTC *Red for Danger*, Sutton Publishing Ltd, Stroud, 1998

Rothnie, Niall *The Baedeker Blitz*, Ian Allan Publishing, Shepperton, 1992

Saward, Graham *Firefighting in Suffolk Volume 1*, own publication, Felixstowe, 1996

Soham Community History Museum *Soham at War*, 2002

Stanistreet, Allan *Brave Railwaymen*, Token Publishing Ltd, Grayshott, 1989

Storey, Neil R *The Lost Coast of Norfolk*, Sutton Publishing, Stroud, 2006

Summers, Dorothy *The East Coast Floods*, David and Charles, Newton Abbot, 1978

Tice, Frank *Tales of the East Coast*, Ian Henry Publications Ltd, Romford, 1995

Williams, David L *British Ferries*, Ian Allan, Hersham, 2003

(2) Newspapers

Bury Free Press
Bury and Norwich Post
Cambridge Chronicle
Cambridge Daily News
Cambridge Evening News
Cambridge Independent Press
Cambs Times
Clacton Gazette
Daily Chronicle
Daily Mail
East Anglian Daily Times
Eastern Daily Press
Eastern Evening News
East Suffolk Gazette
Ely Standard
Essex Herald
Essex Weekly News
Evening Star
Hunts Post
London Daily News and Leader

London Gazette
Lynn News
Morning Chronicle
Newmarket Journal
Norfolk Chronicle
Norfolk News
Norwich Evening News
Norwich Mercury
Peterborough Evening Telegraph
Peterborough Standard
The Times
Yarmouth Mercury

Index